50 State Odyssey from Sea to Shining Sea

An Amateur Photographer's Perspective

Paul M Ingevaldson

Published by Gary Slavin, Longwood, Florida
© 2017 by Paul M. Ingevaldson
Printed in the United States of America

ISBN: 978-0-692-96332-6

Library of Congress Control Number: 2017956824

Format and Layout by Carolyn Sheltraw

This paper meets the requirements of ANSI/NISO Z39.48-1992 (Permanence of Paper).

www.paulingevaldson.com

About this book

This book will take the reader on a tour of our beautiful country showing a picture of something famous that represents that state. The cover represents the four regions of the United States, namely the West, the South, the Midwest and the East

Cover clockwise:
Yellowstone Falls - Wyoming
Hemingway Home - Key West, Florida
Old Water Tower & John Hancock Building - Chicago
Entrance to Baseball Hall of Fame - NY

An Amateur Photographer's Journey from Sea to Shining Sea

My project to experience and photograph places and things across our country was a very rewarding effort. My goal was to take pictures that represented all that is America. You will see pictures that represent our involvement in our foreign and domestic wars as well as pictures that display our national resources. There will be pictures about some of our sports and one picture of the impact of a terrorist attack in Oklahoma City. There are pictures that display the beautiful places in our country including swamps, canyons, waterfalls, an active volcano, glaciers and mountains as well as pictures depicting discoveries of our earliest explorers. You will see entertainment venues along with some of our native wildlife. You will see beautiful grand hotels, a bed and breakfast and a beautiful old home in Pennsylvania where my mother and her 11 siblings spent their childhood. There are pictures representing American history and there are pictures representing many iconic places throughout our beautiful country. You will see our two oceans, our mightiest river and two of our Great Lakes. You will see where manned flight began, where ice cream is made, where Tennessee whiskey is distilled and where cotton and potatoes are grown.

This grand tour has been very inspiring in this time of domestic and international strife. Our country is breathtaking, varied and unique. Hopefully you will enjoy this journey as much as my wife and I enjoyed experiencing it.

Paul M. Ingevaldson

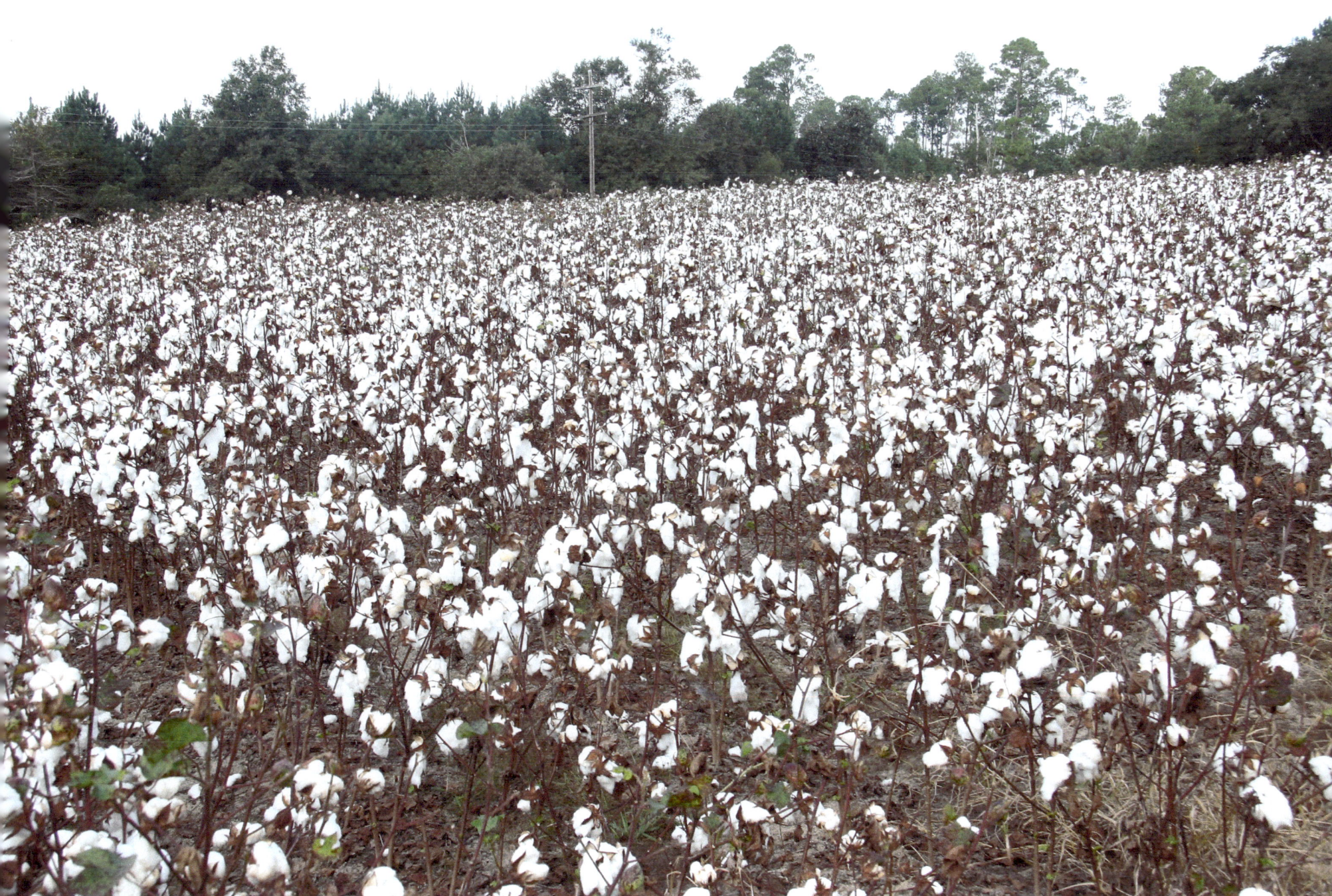

Alabama-King Cotton

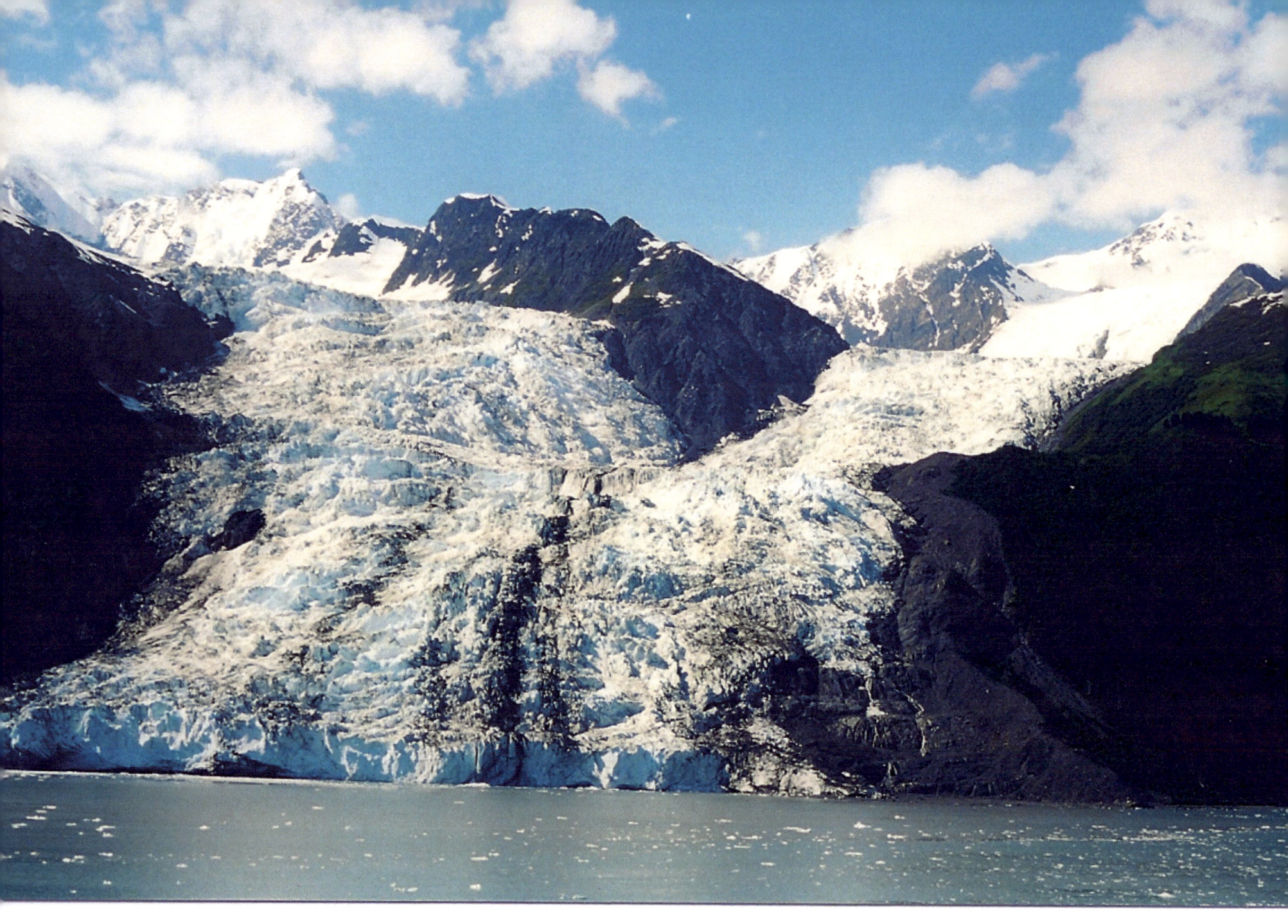

Alaska-Bryn Mawr Glacier within College Fjord

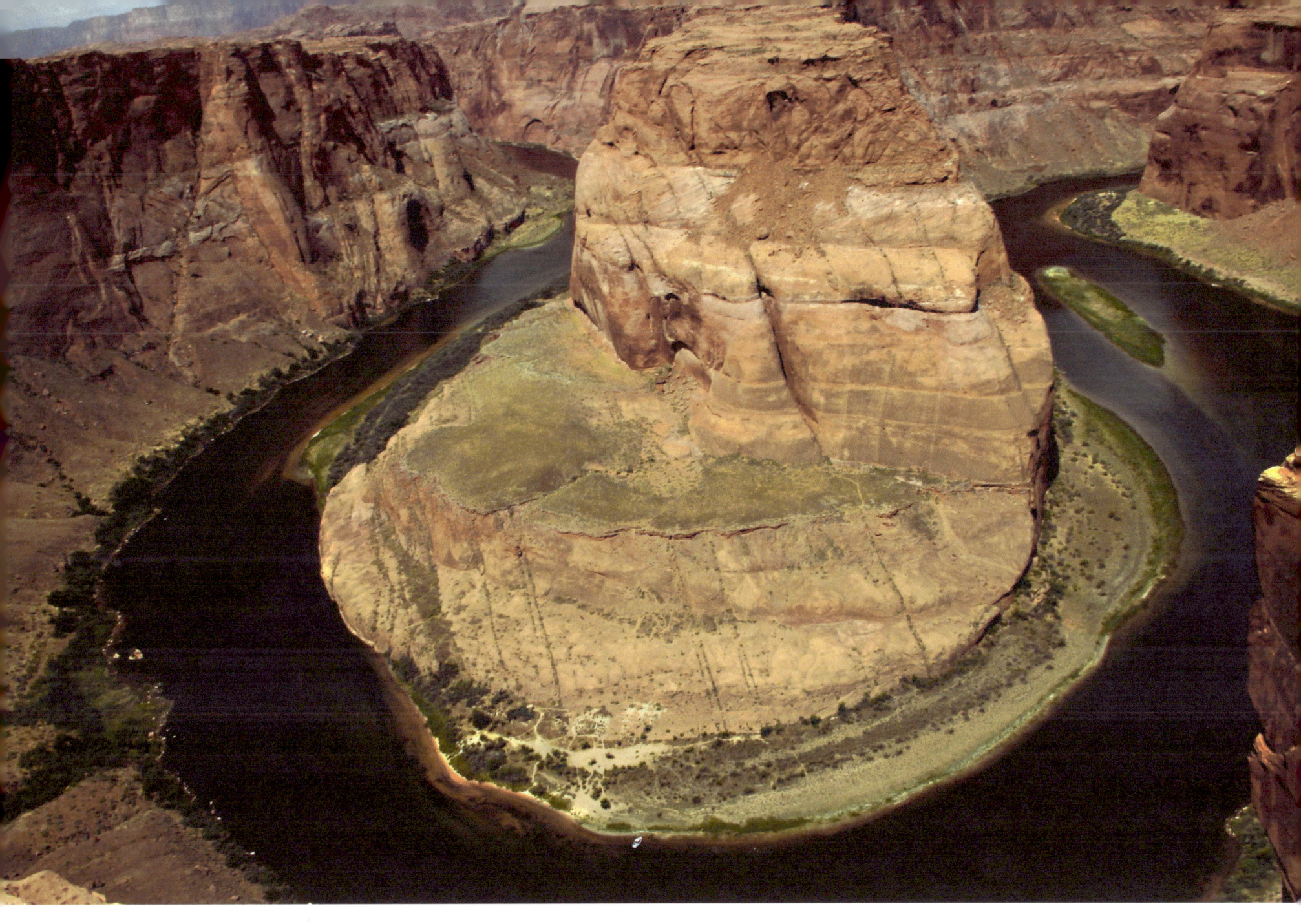

Arizona-Horseshoe Bend of the Colorado River-near Page

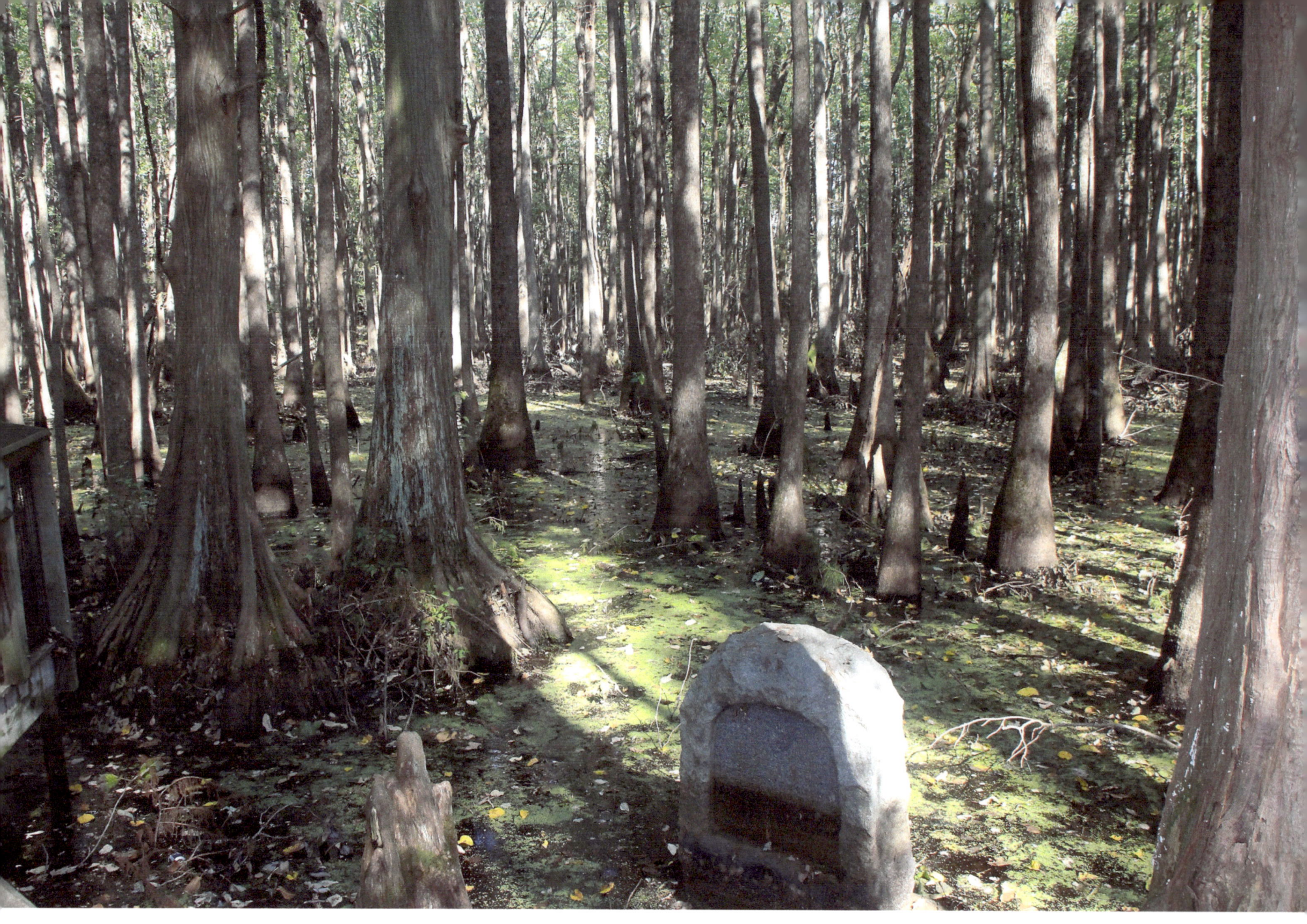

Arkansas-Cypress swamp with monument showing where the survey for the Louisiana Purchase began

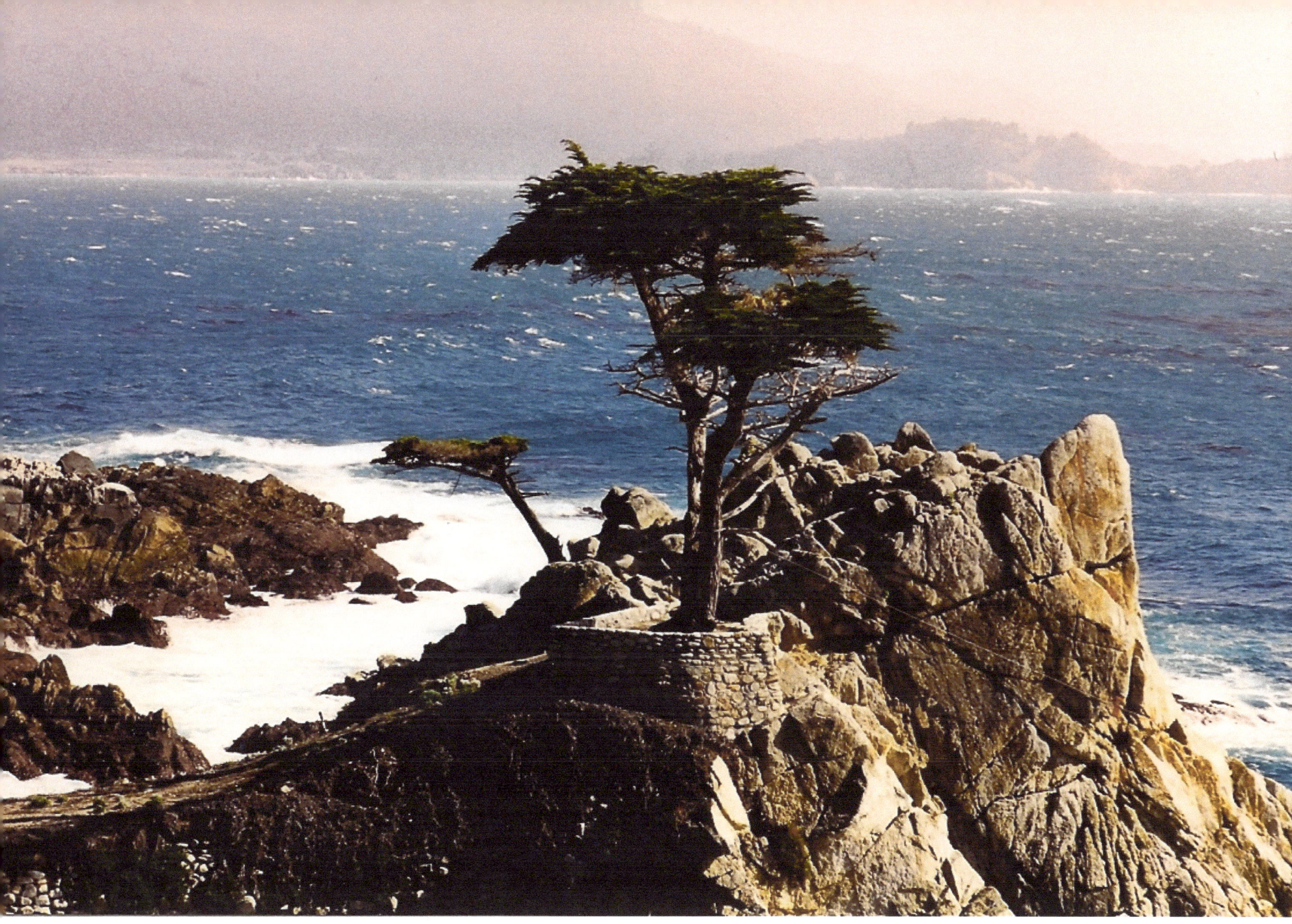

California-Lone Cypress-Near Pebble Beach

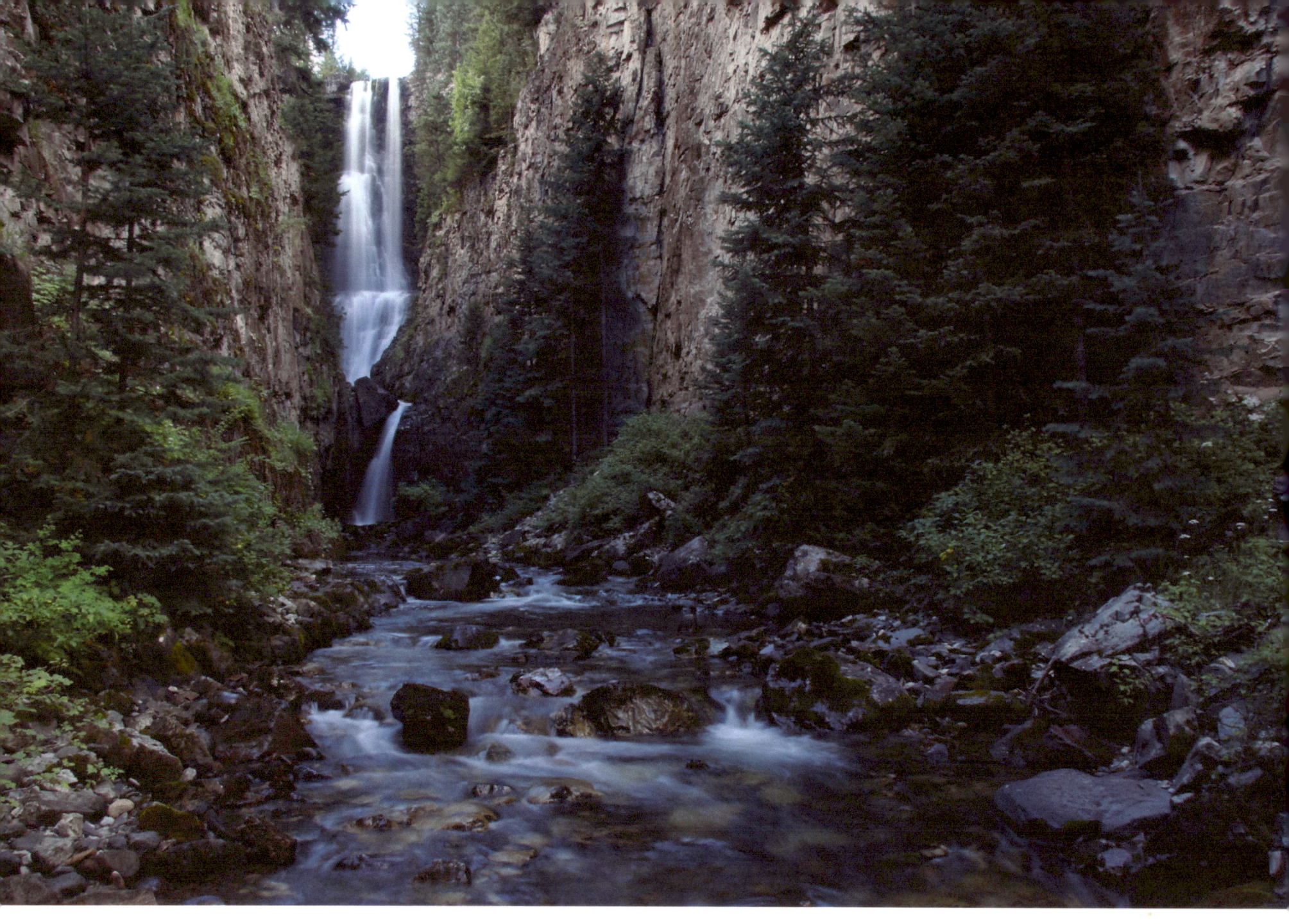

Colorado-Mystic Falls near Telluride

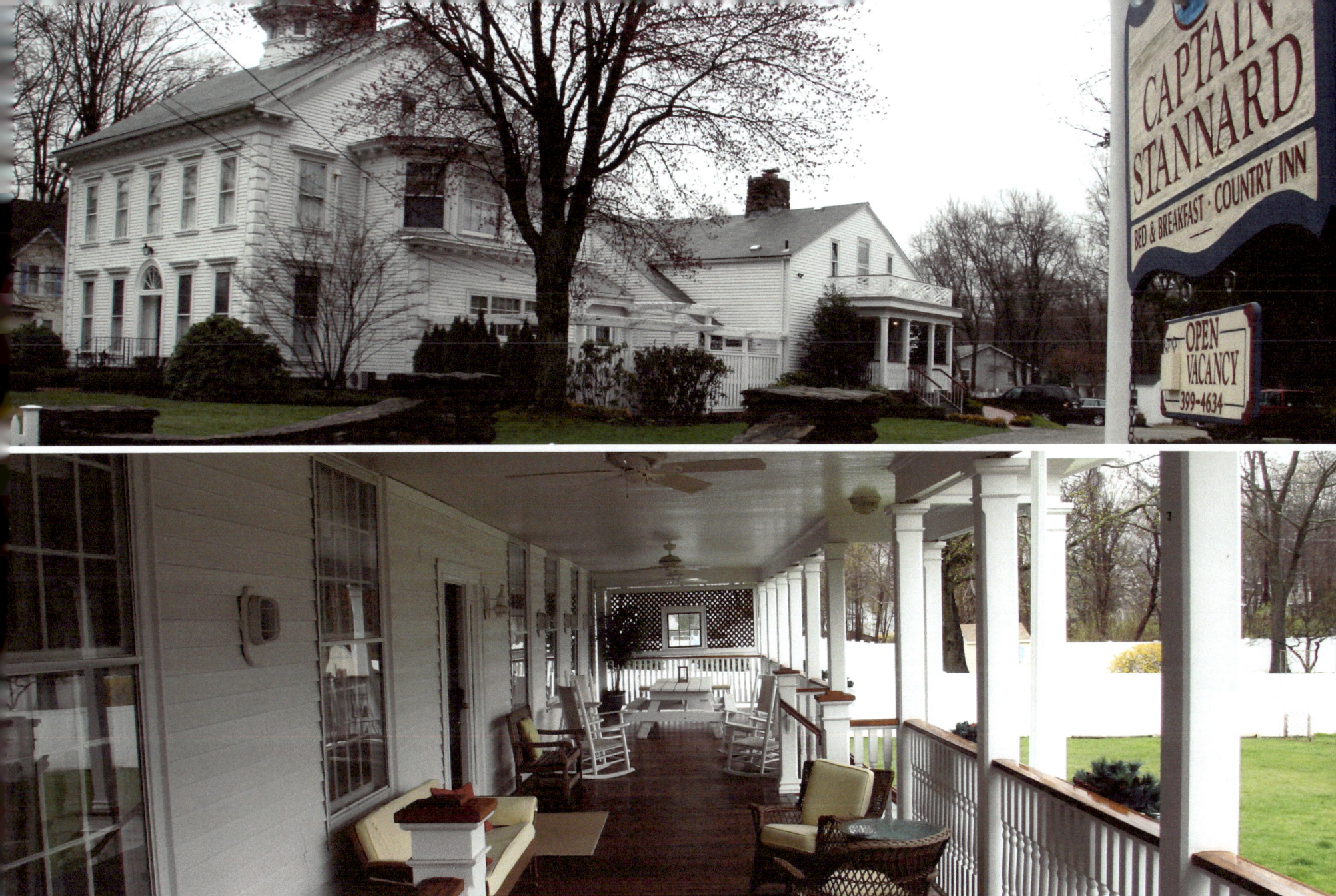

Connecticut-Captain Stannard Bed and Breakfast-Westbrook

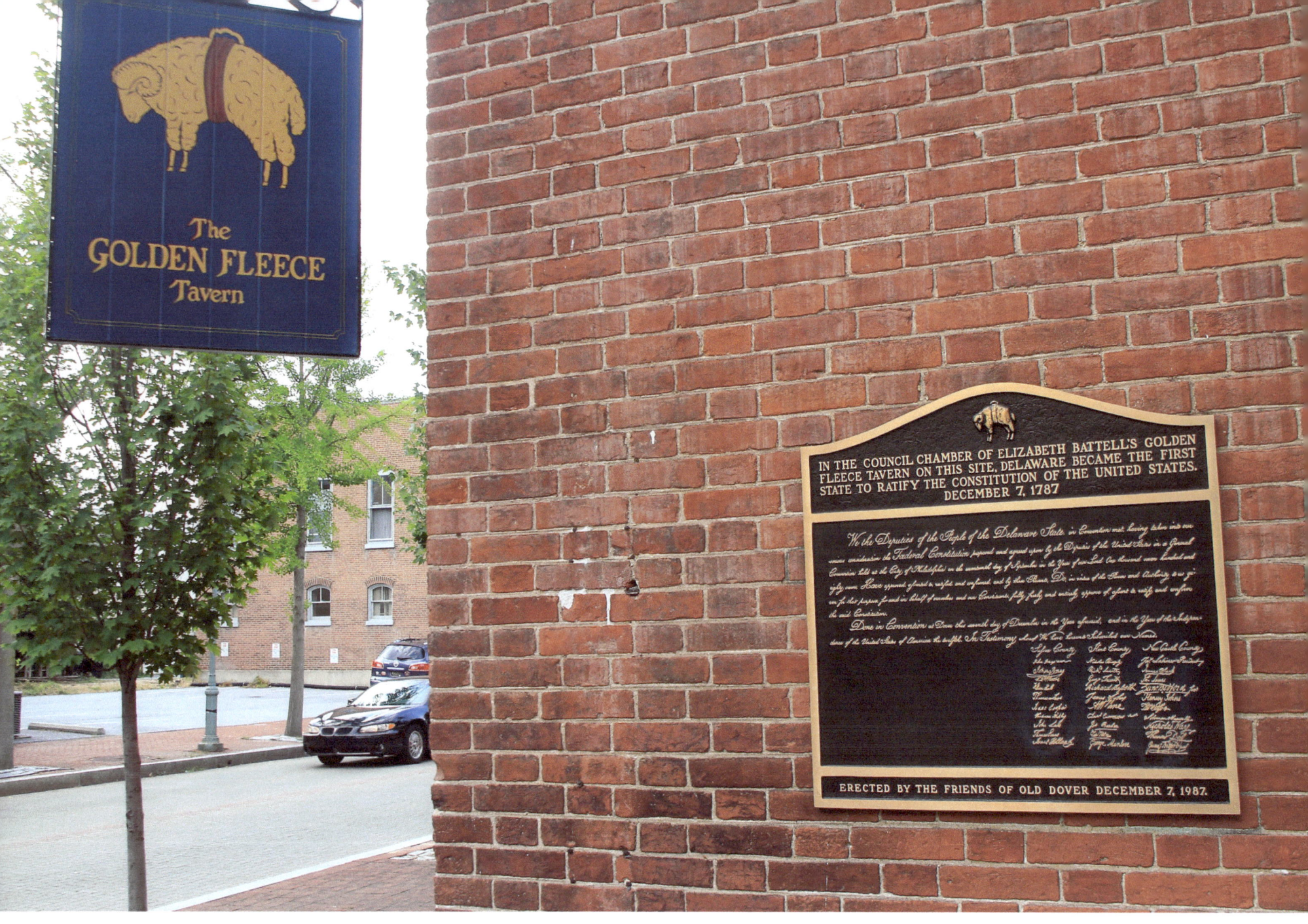

Delaware-Site in Dover, Delaware where officials were the first State Assembly to ratify the Constitution.

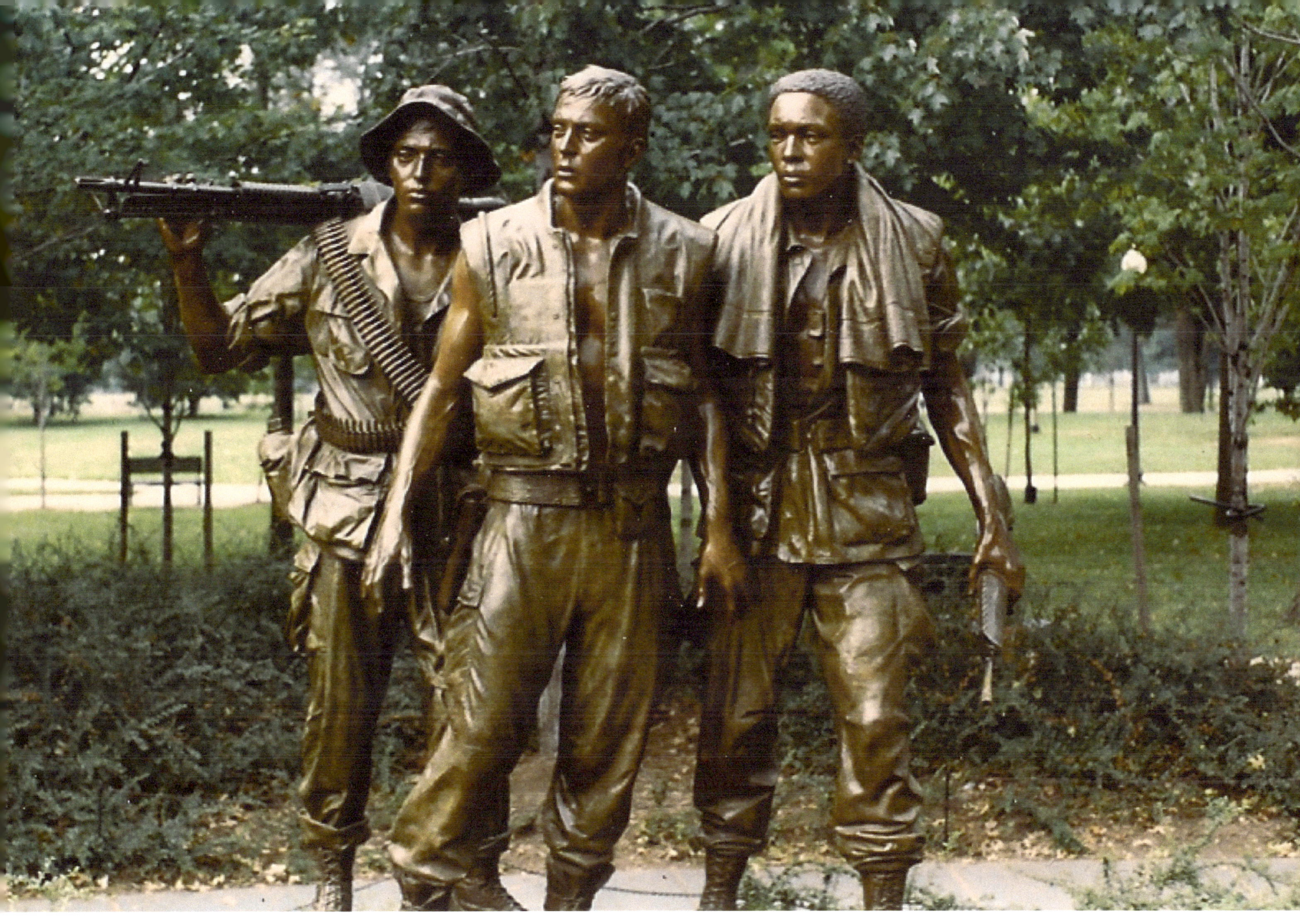

District of Columbia-Vietnam Statue

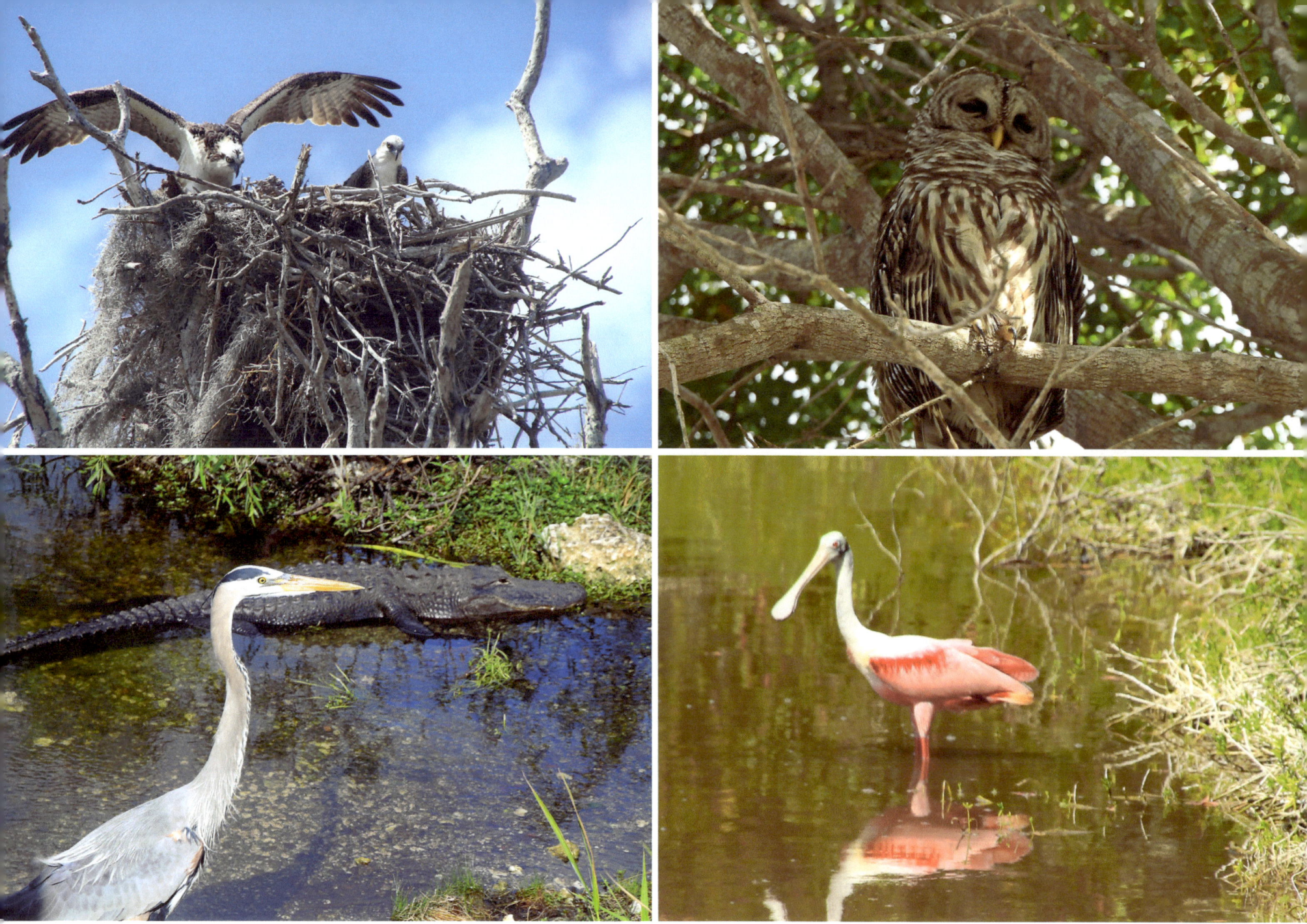

Florida-Birds of the Everglades plus an alligator

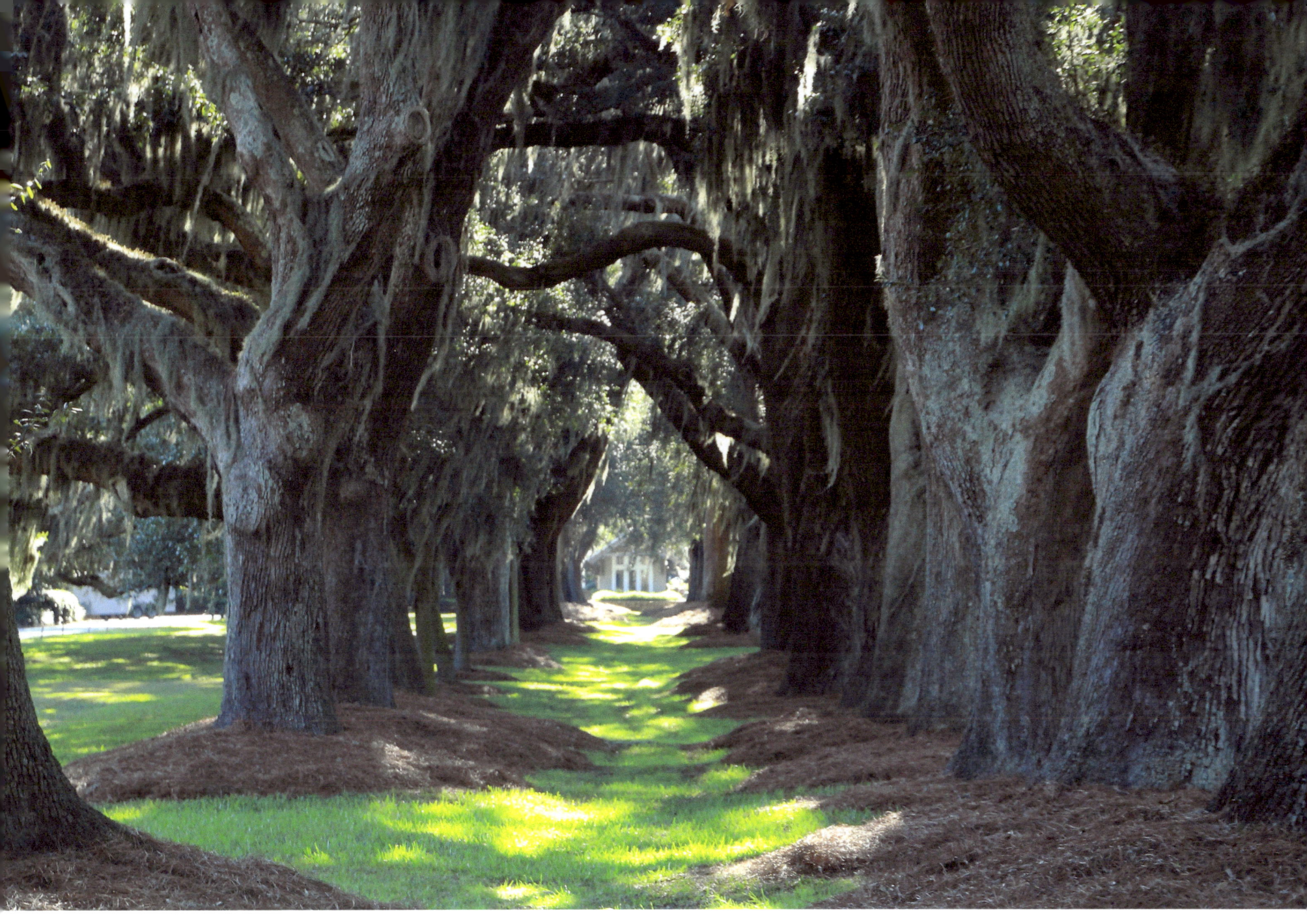

Georgia-Entrance to The Lodge in the Sea Island Resort

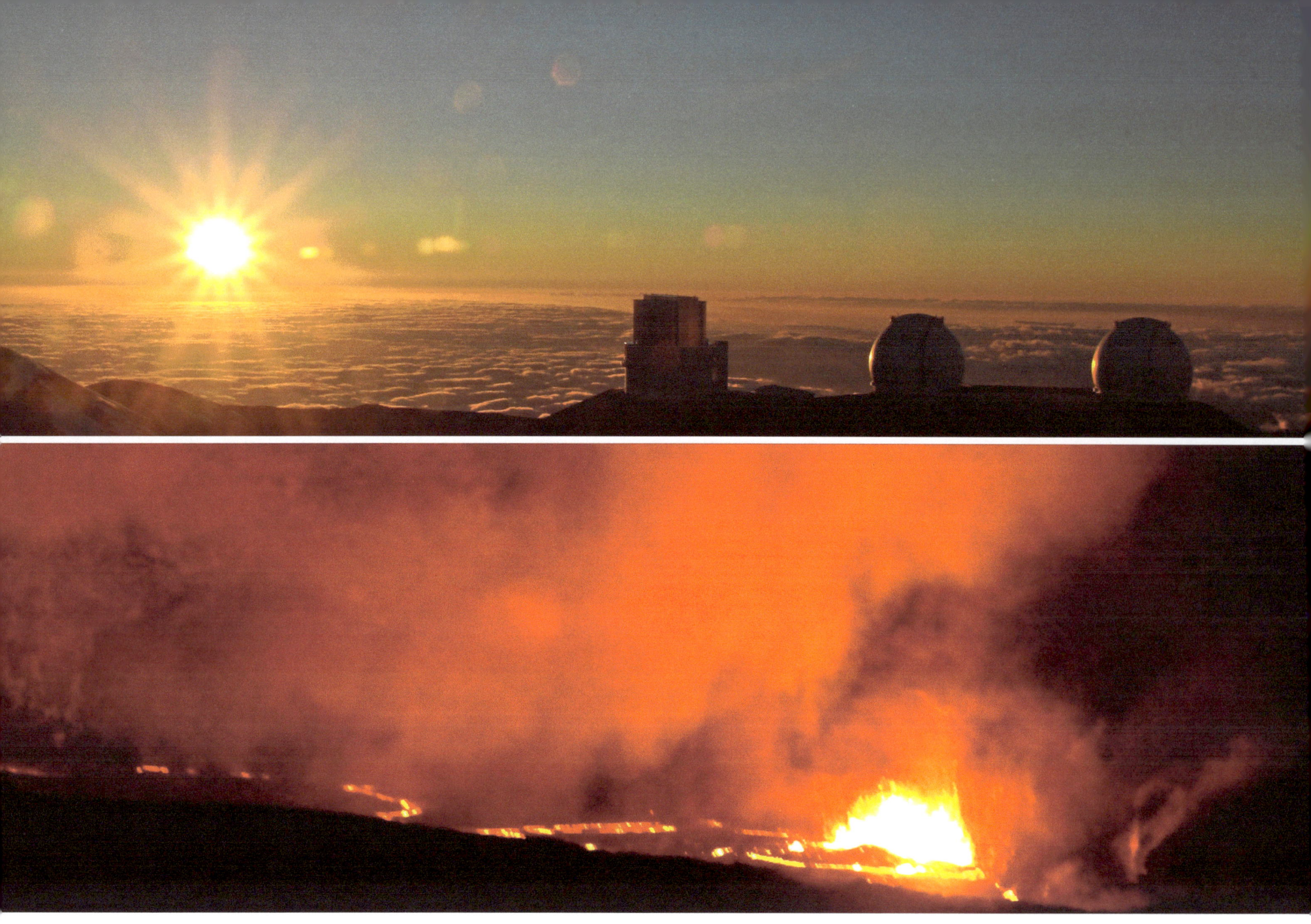

Hawaii-Top-Sunset atop Mauna Kea-Bottom-The Kilaeua caldera at night

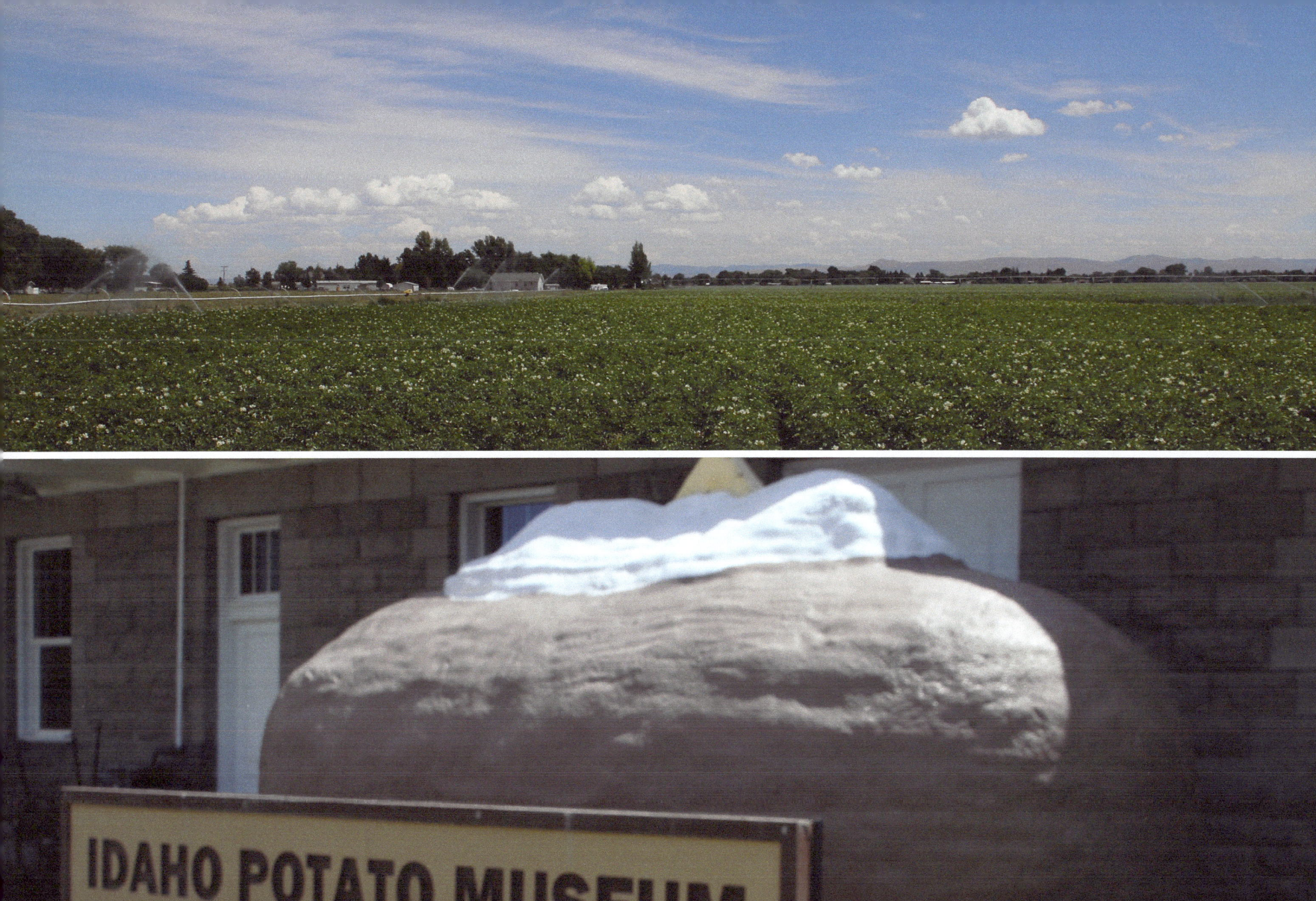

Idaho-Potato Country-Blackfoot

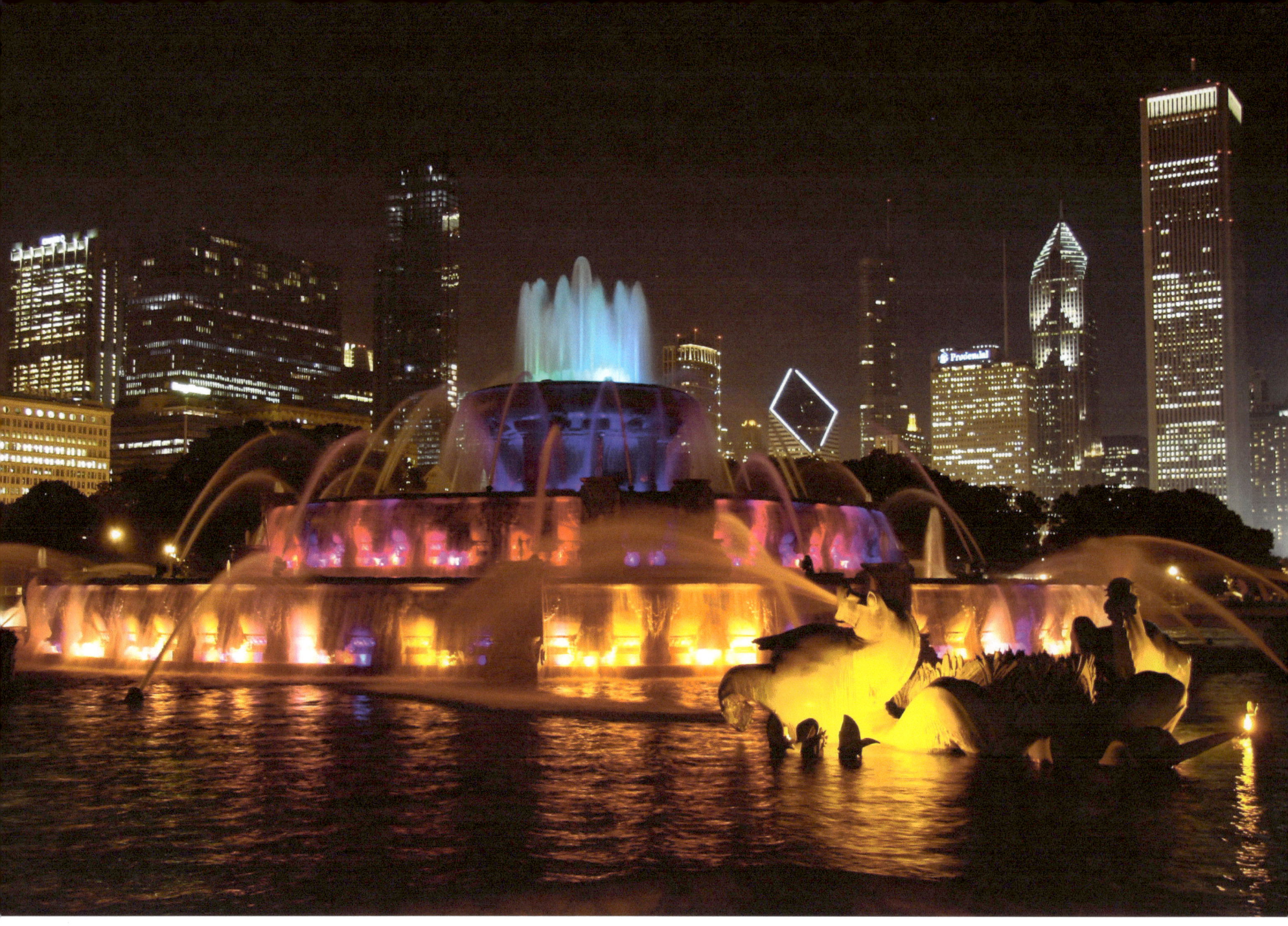

Illinois-Buckingham Fountain at night-Chicago

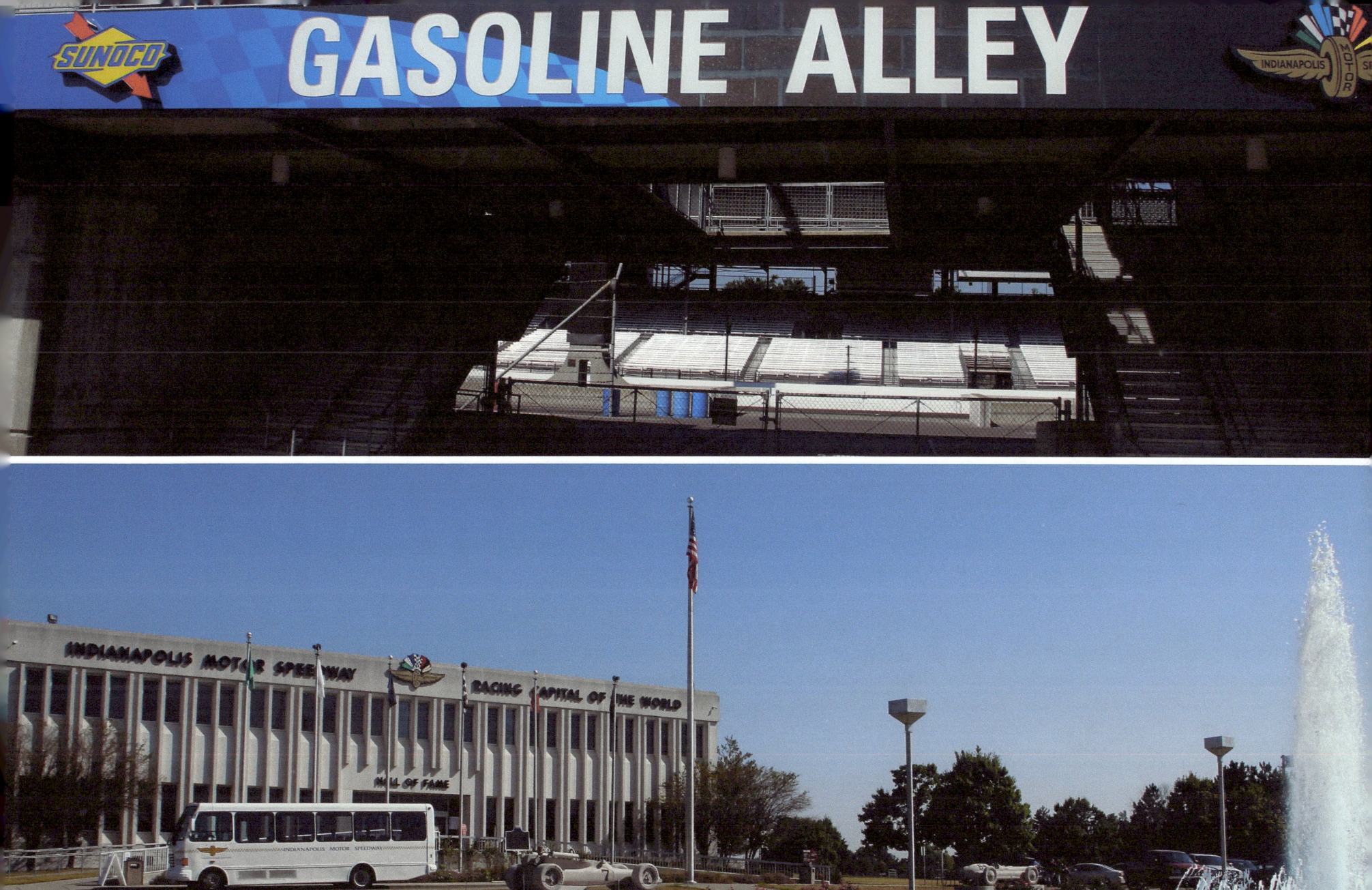

Indiana-Indy-The Greatest Spectacle in Racing-Indianapolis

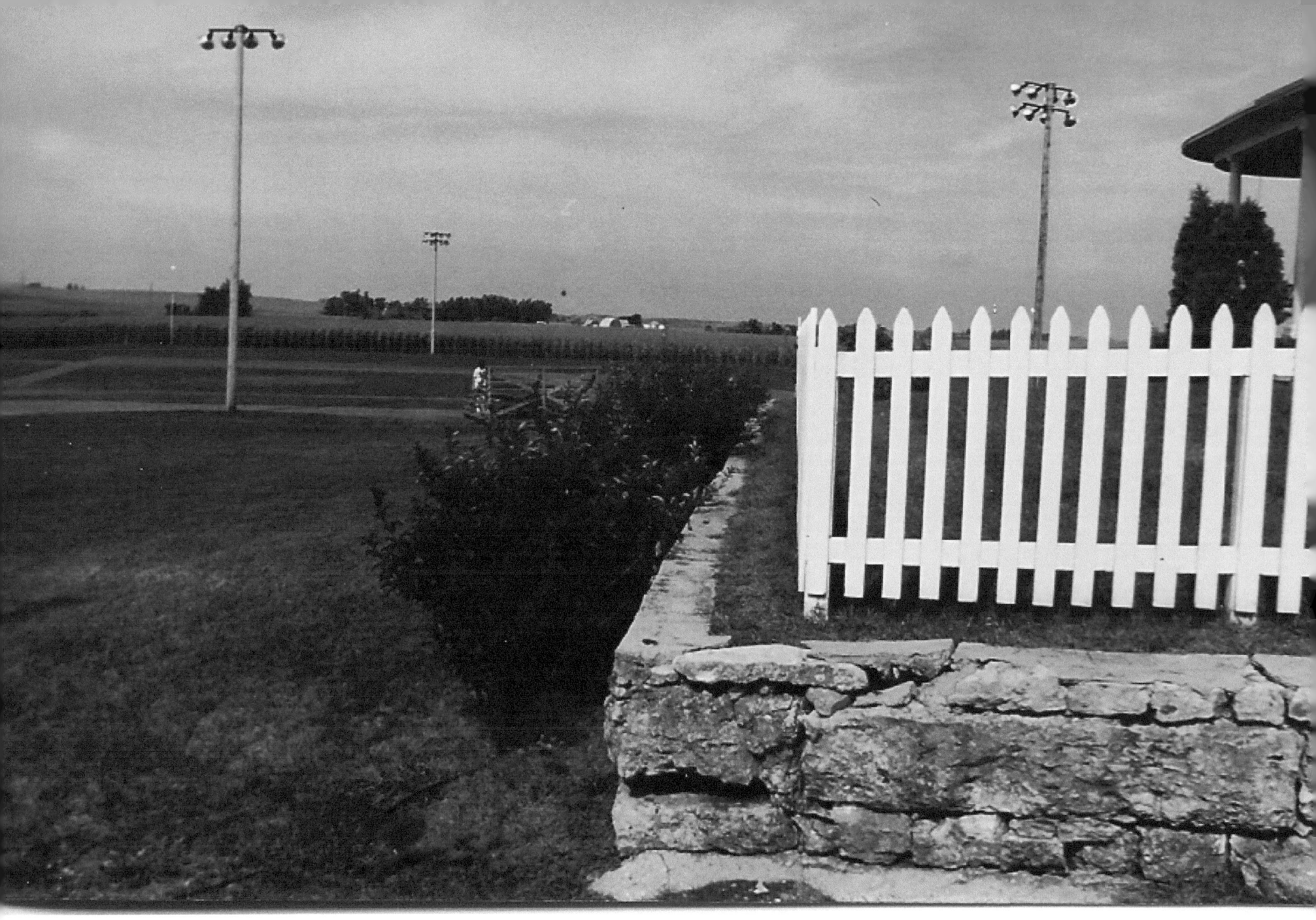

Iowa-Field Of Dreams-"Build It and They Will Come"-Dyersville

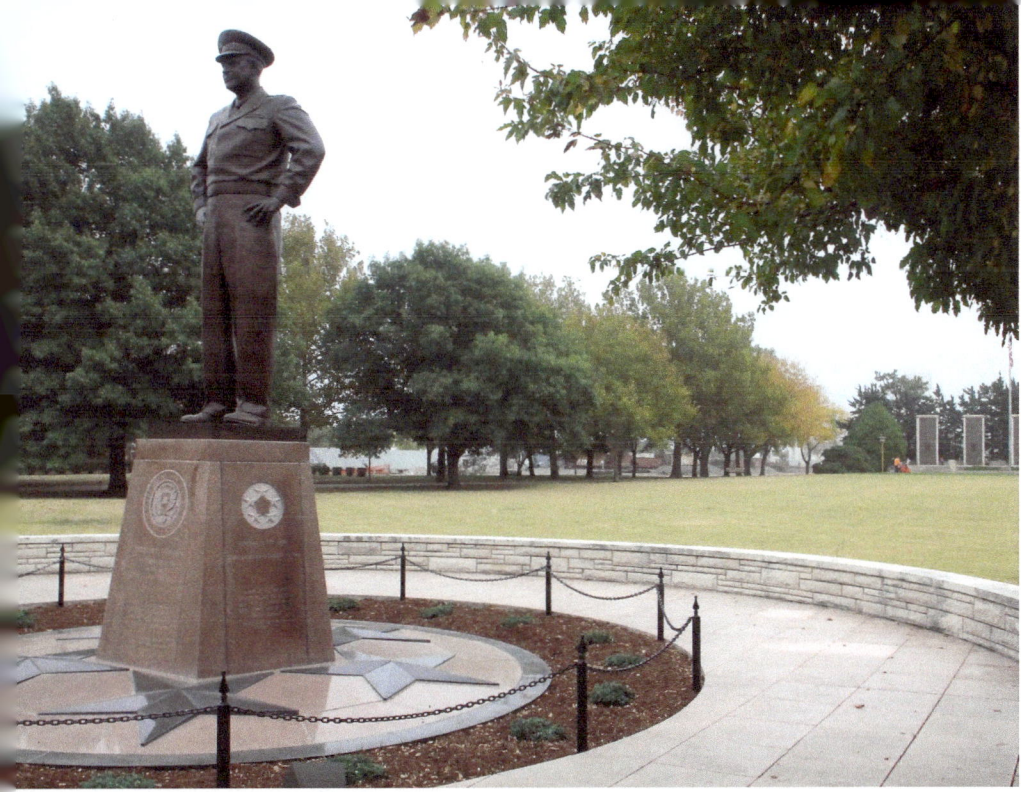

Kansas-Dwight D Eisenhower

Statue and Boyhood home-Abilene

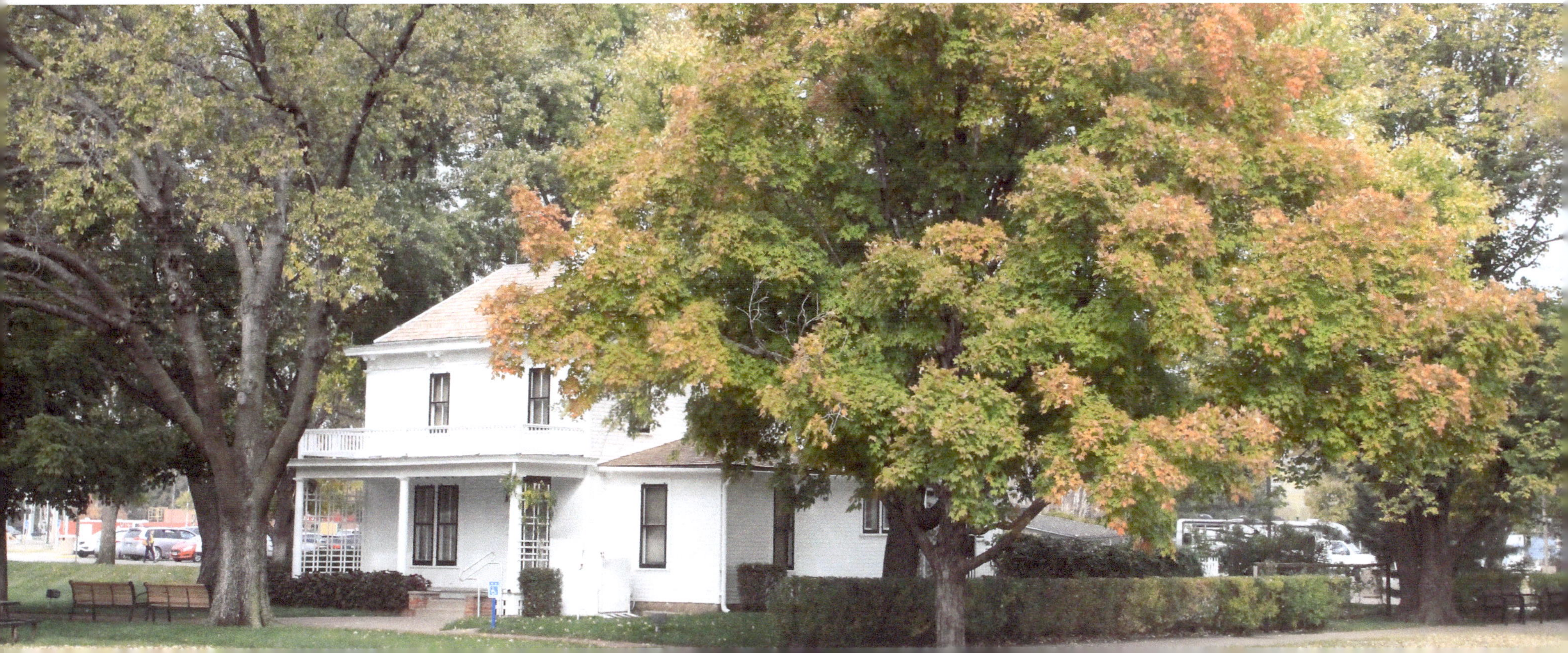

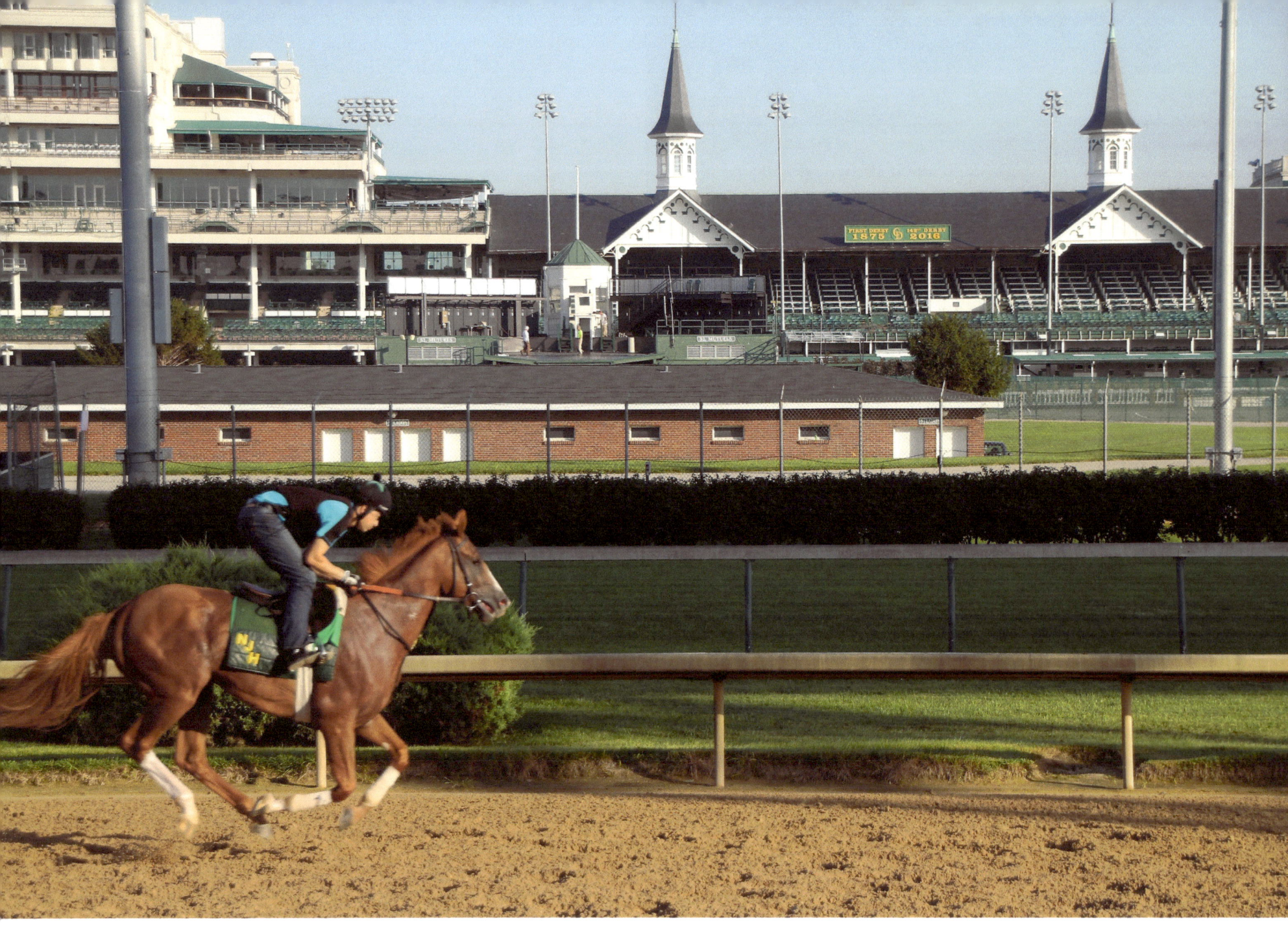

Kentucky-Airborne on the back stretch-Churchill Downs-Louisville

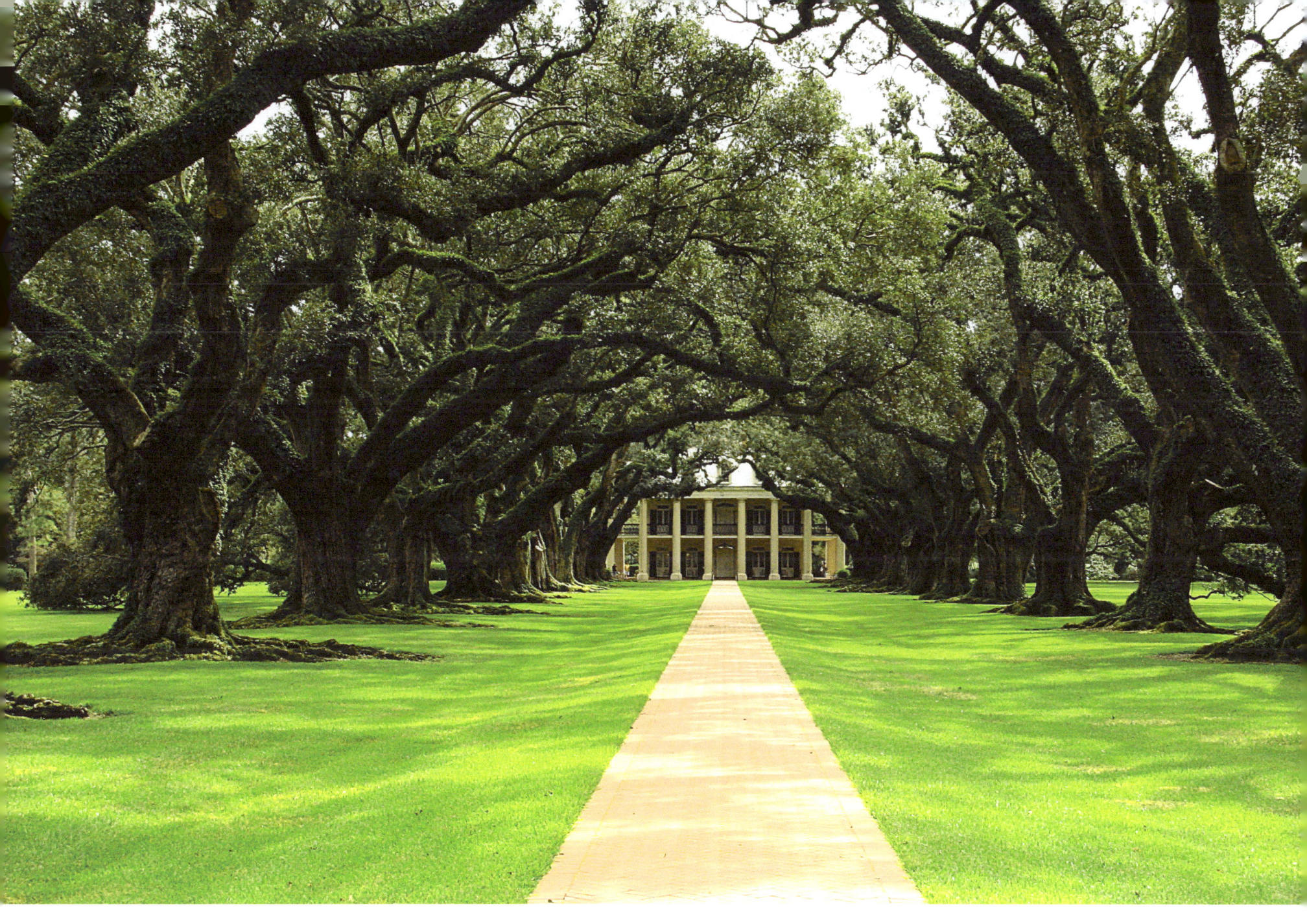

Louisiana-Oak Alley Sugar Plantation-Vacherie

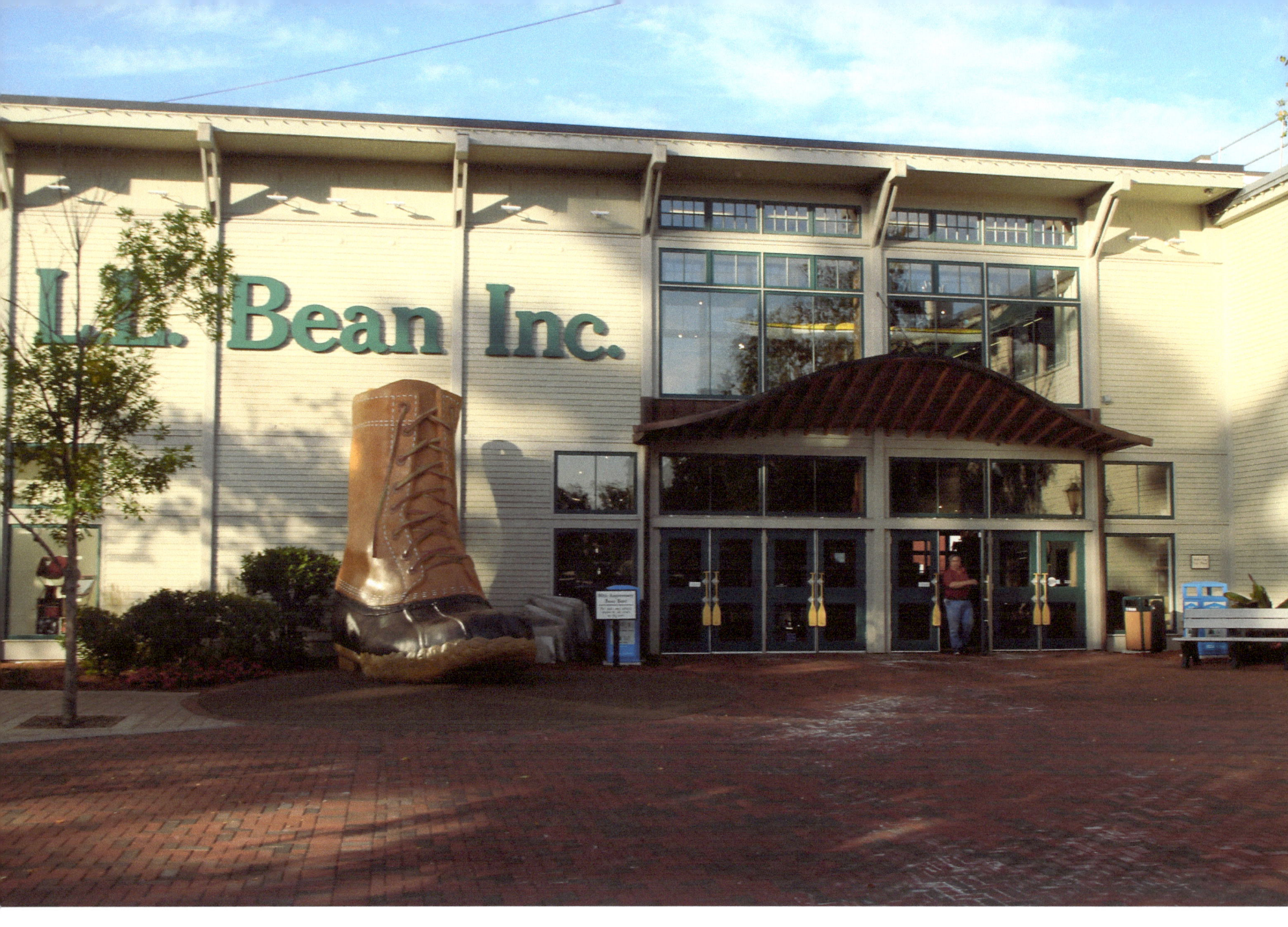

Maine-L.L. Bean Flagship Store-Freeport

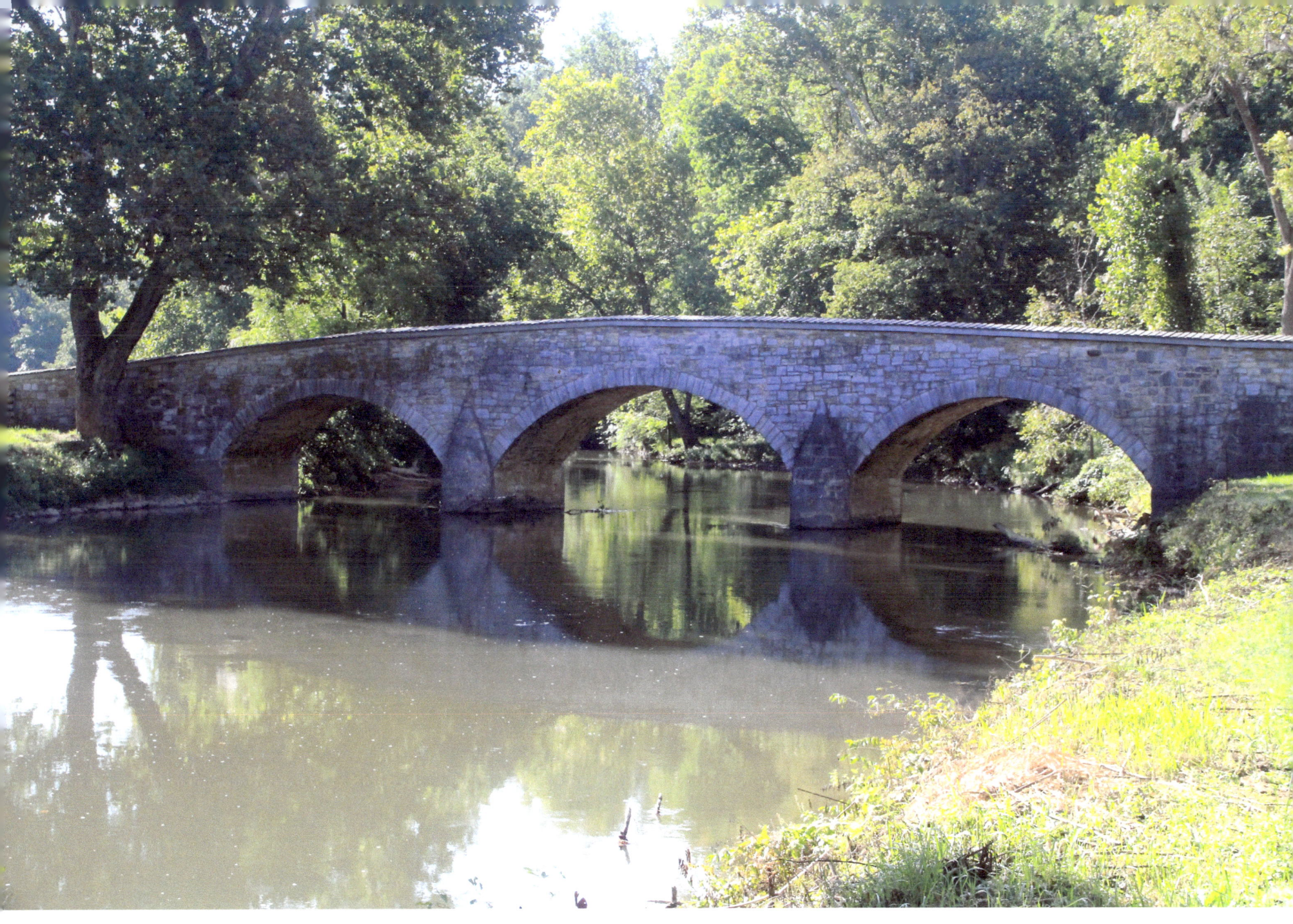

Maryland-Burnside's Bridge-Antietam Battlefield-This battle lasted one day resulting in 22,750 American casualties, the bloodiest day in American military history.

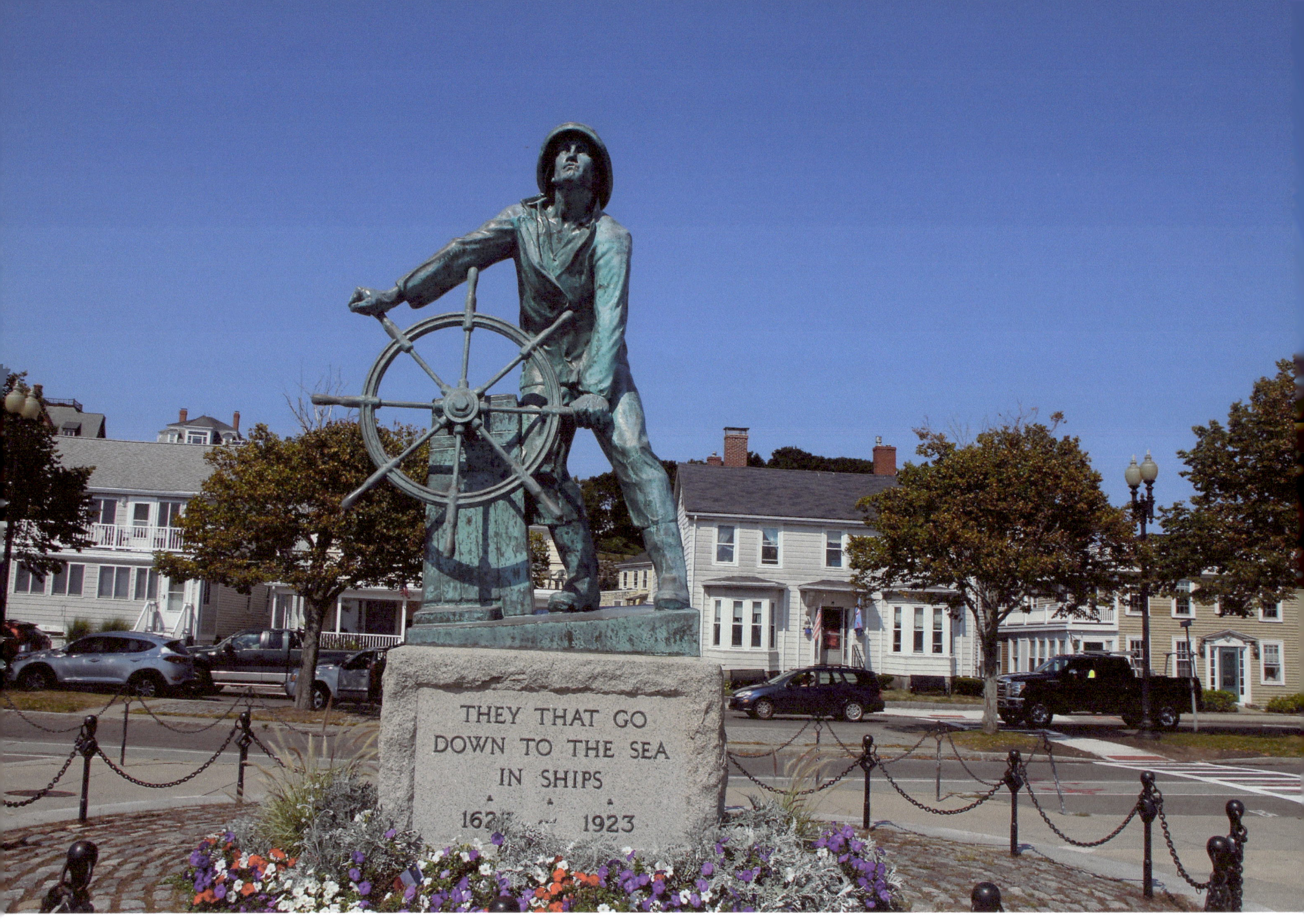

THEY THAT GO
DOWN TO THE SEA
IN SHIPS
1623 ⚓ 1923

Massachusetts-The Fisherman's Memorial-Gloucester-It commemorates Gloucester fishermen lost at sea.

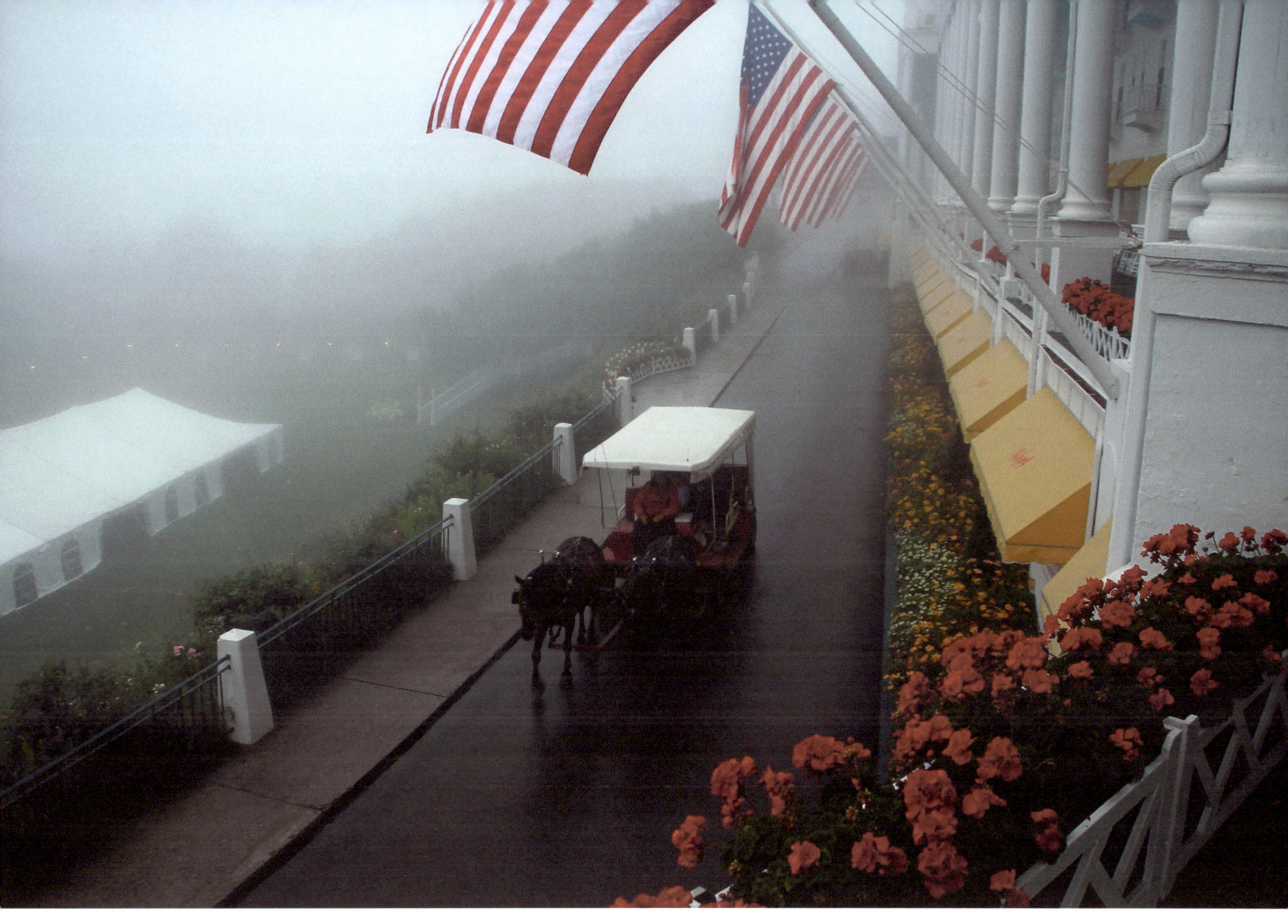

Michigan-Grand Hotel-Mackinac Island-Morning Taxi Service

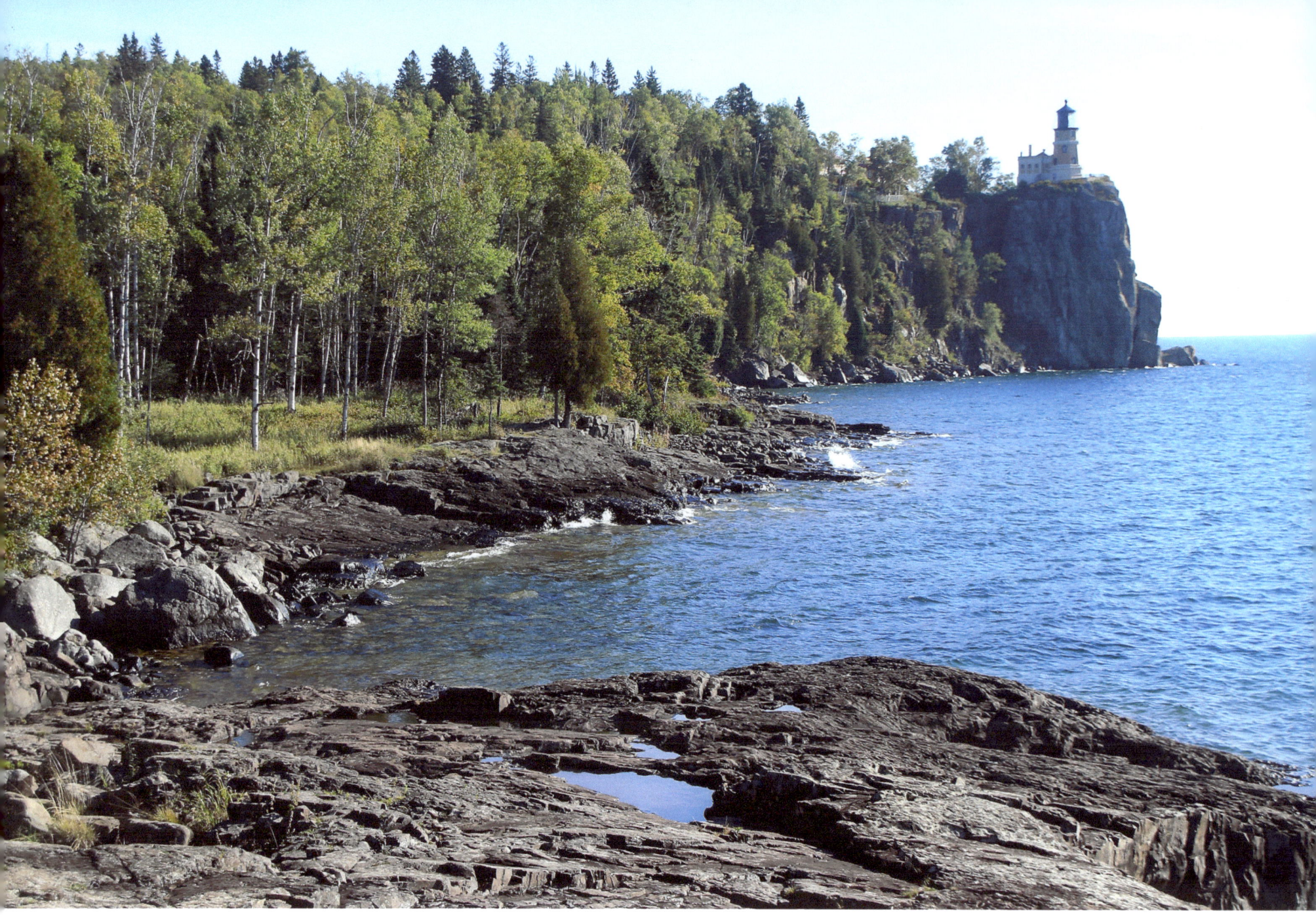

Minnesota-Split Rock Lighthouse on Lake Superior. Near Duluth

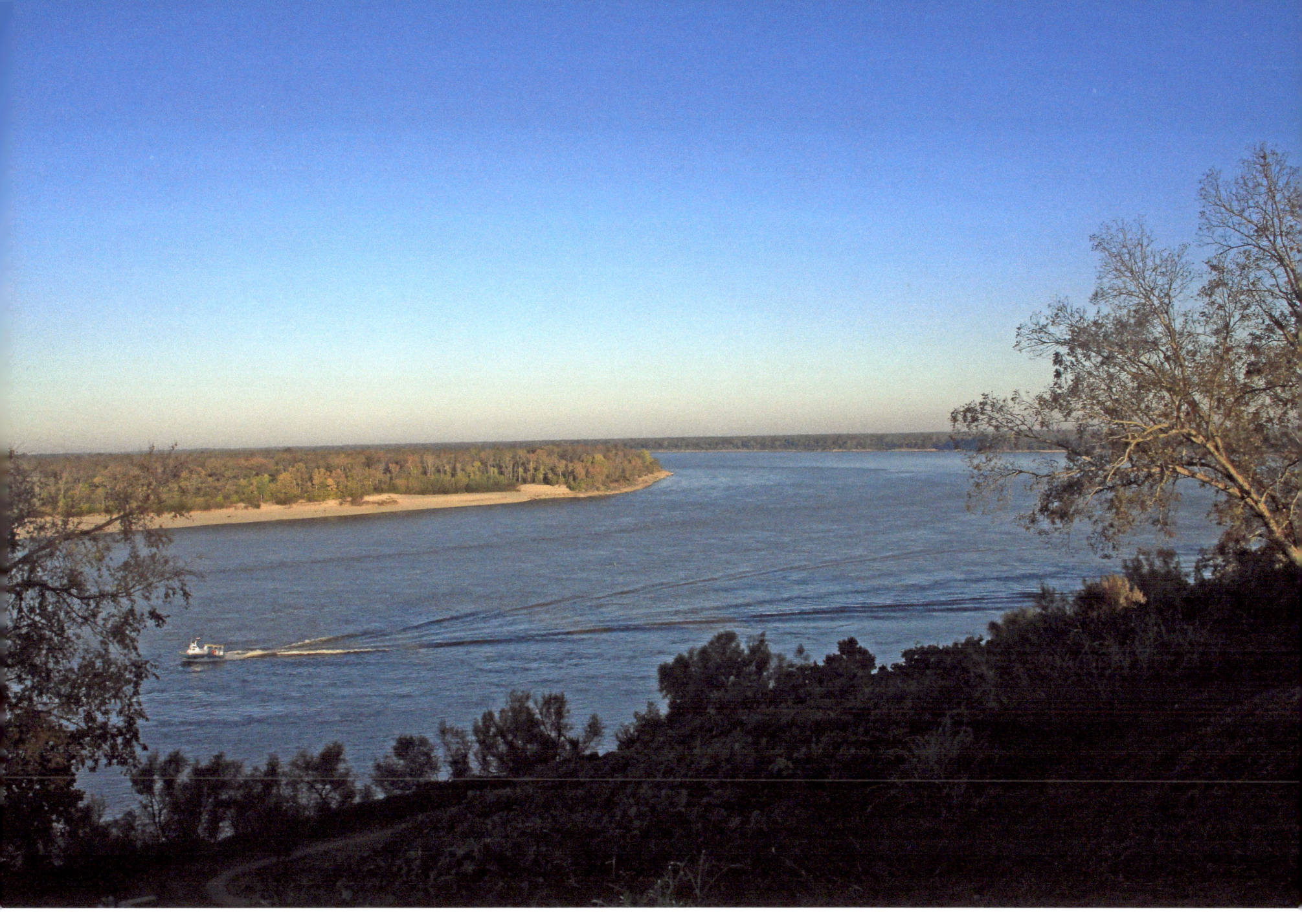

Mississippi-Looking across the Mississippi to Arkansas from Vicksburg Battlefield

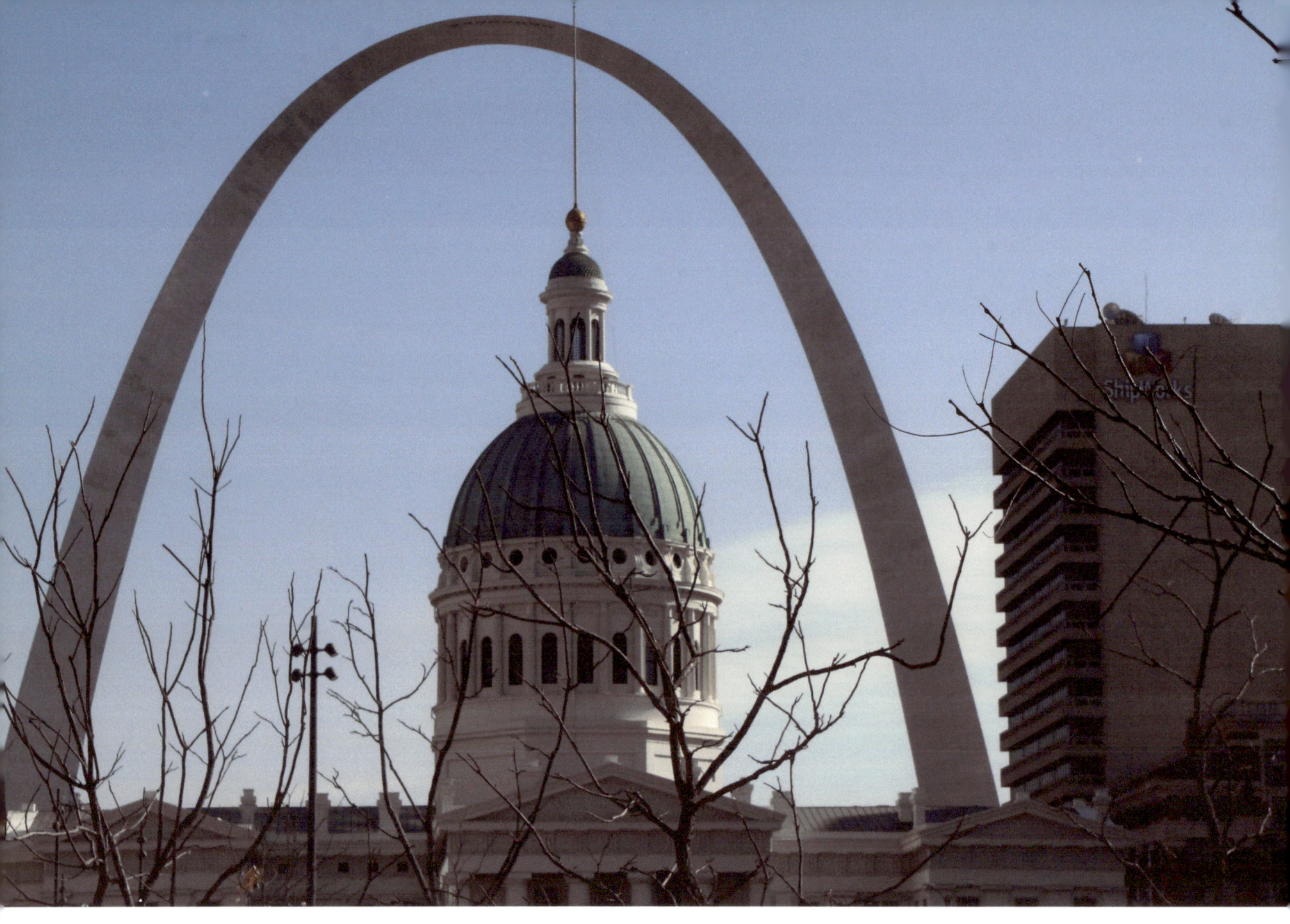

Missouri-St. Louis Gateway Arch and the Old State House

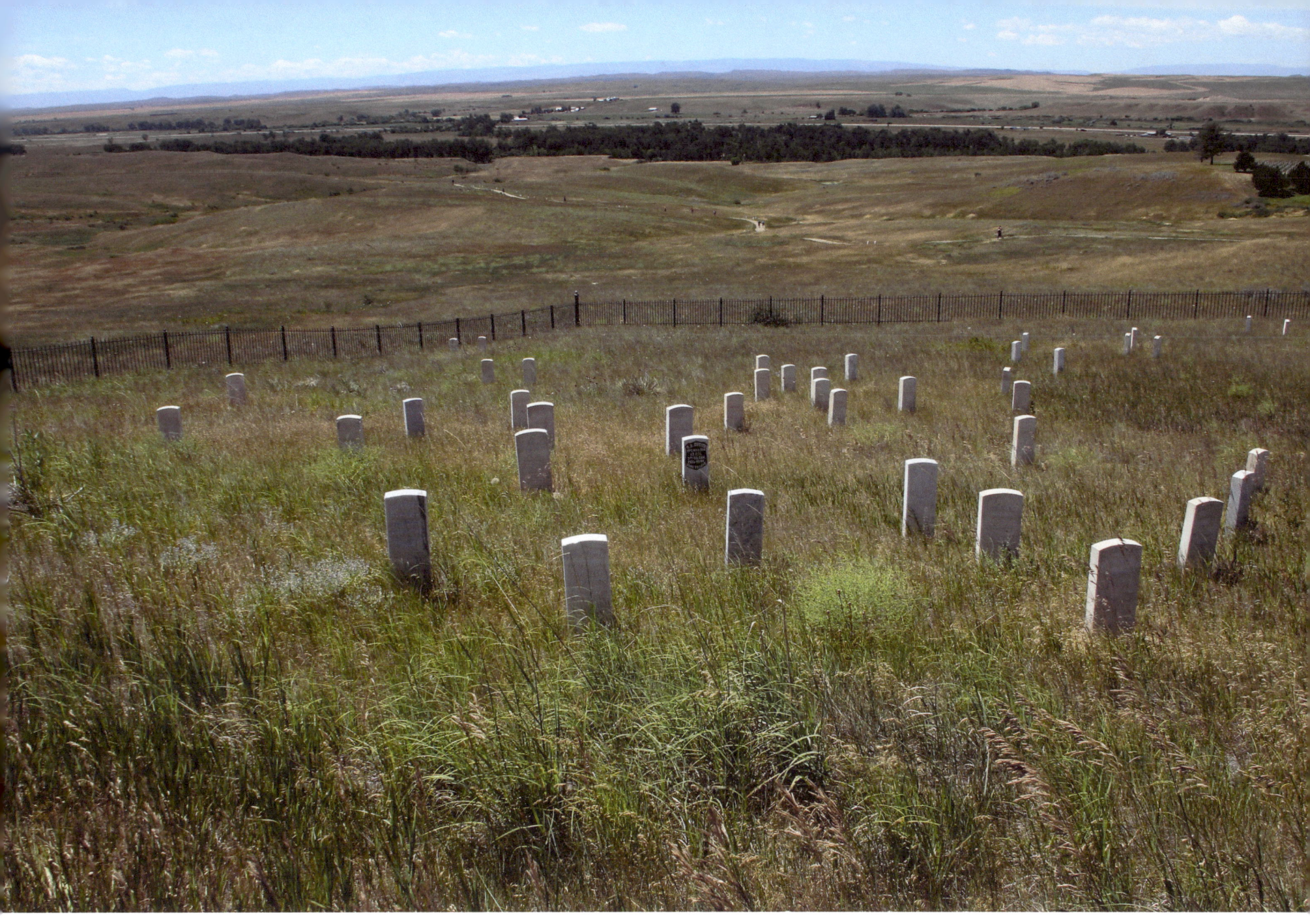

Montana-This is the actual battlefield where the 7th Cavalry was defeated by the Oglala Lakota Sioux Indians led by Crazy Horse. The monuments denote where they fell. Custer's is in black.

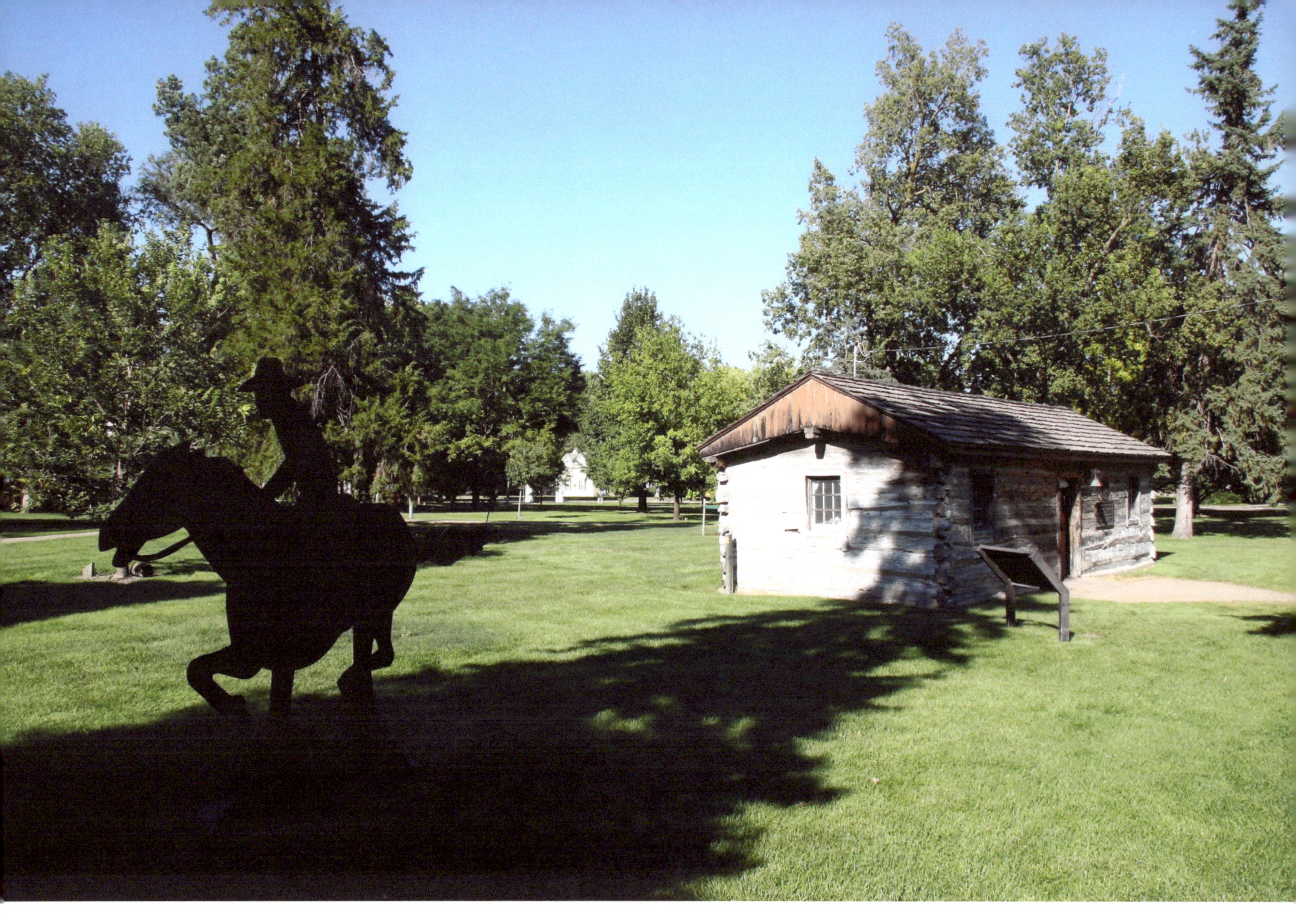

Nebraska-Pony Express Station-Gothenburg-The Pony Express was in existence for only 18 months.

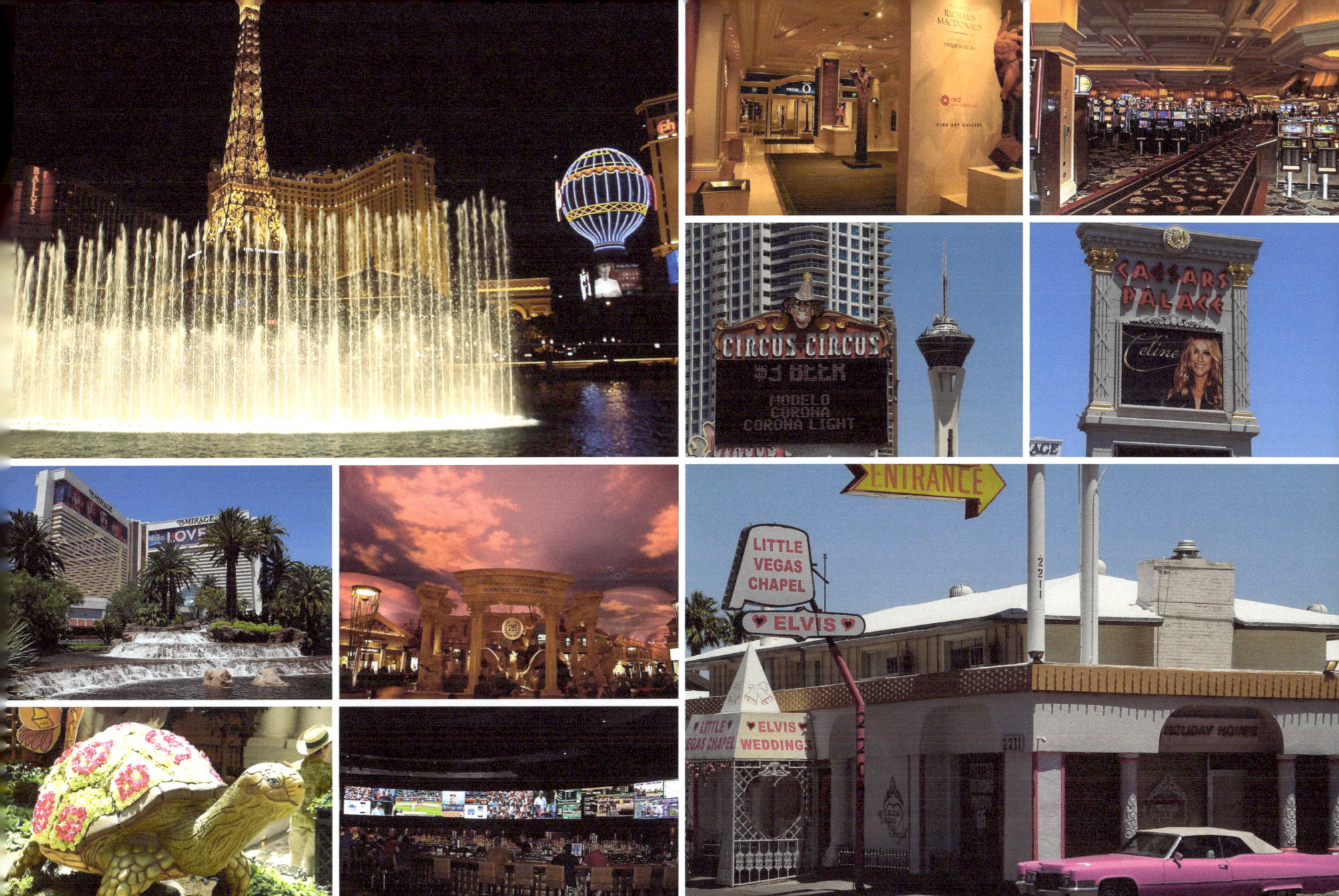

Nevada-Las Vegas

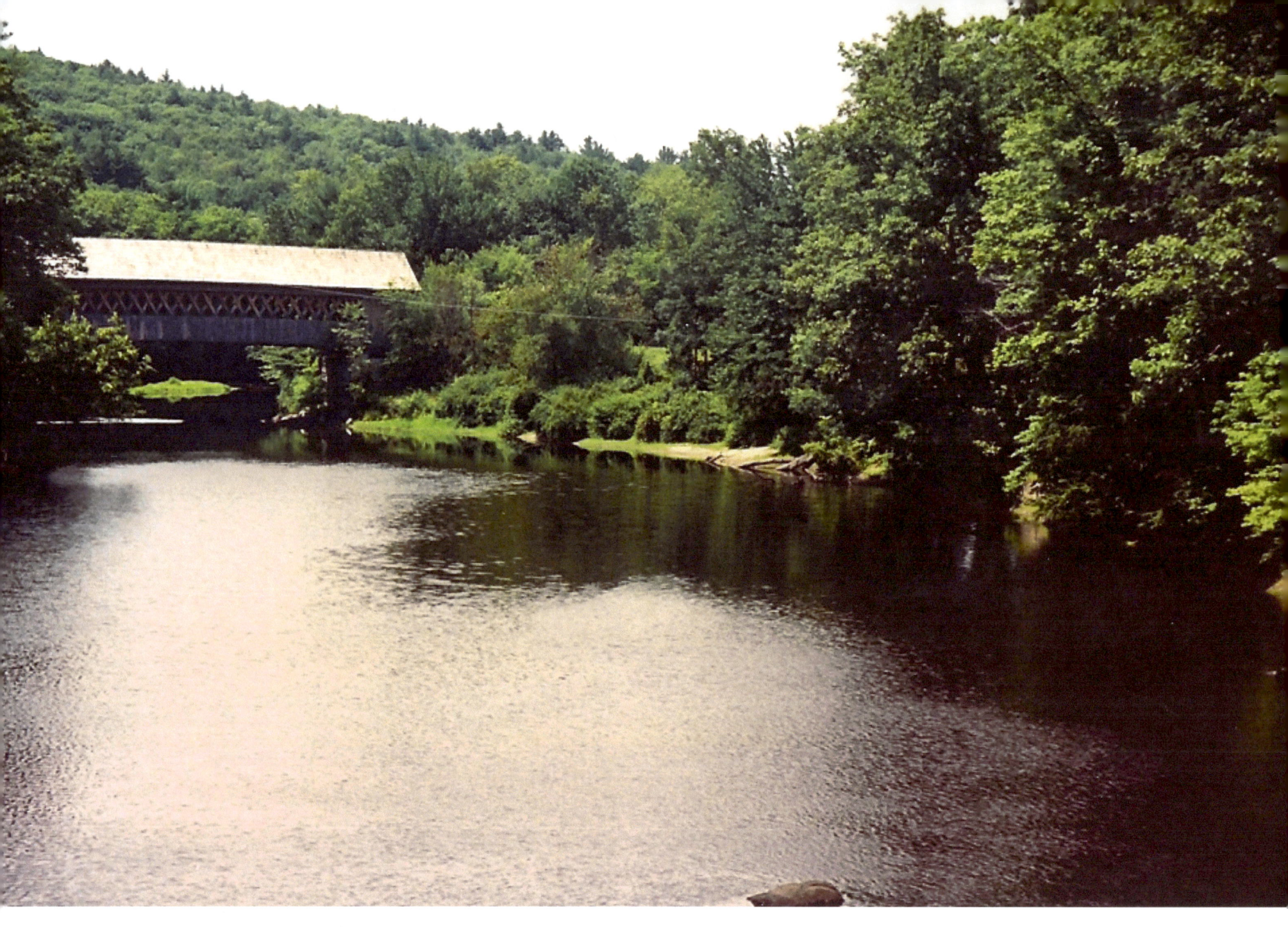

New Hampshire-Covered Bridge- New England College-Henniker

New Jersey

Where Washington Crossed the Delaware River from Pennsylvania to New Jersey near Trenton

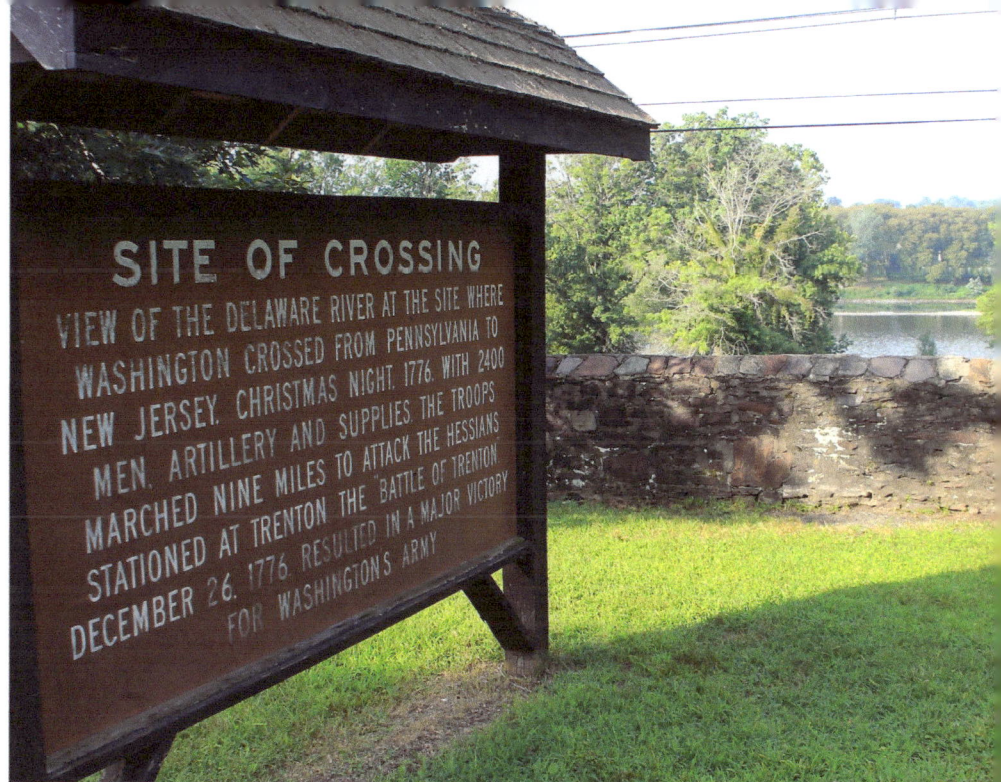

SITE OF CROSSING
VIEW OF THE DELAWARE RIVER AT THE SITE WHERE
WASHINGTON CROSSED FROM PENNSYLVANIA TO
NEW JERSEY, CHRISTMAS NIGHT, 1776, WITH 2400
MEN, ARTILLERY AND SUPPLIES THE TROOPS
MARCHED NINE MILES TO ATTACK THE HESSIANS
STATIONED AT TRENTON THE "BATTLE OF TRENTON"
DECEMBER 26, 1776, RESULTED IN A MAJOR VICTORY
FOR WASHINGTON'S ARMY

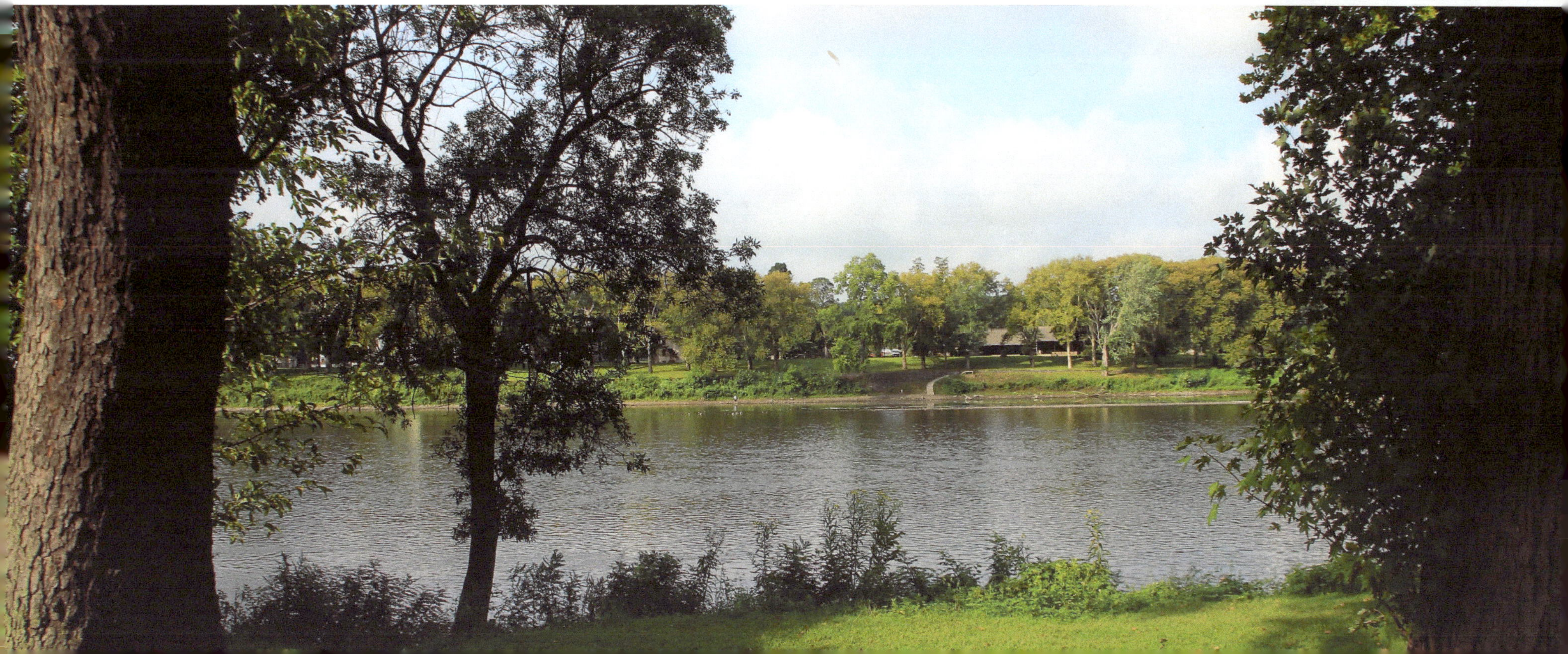

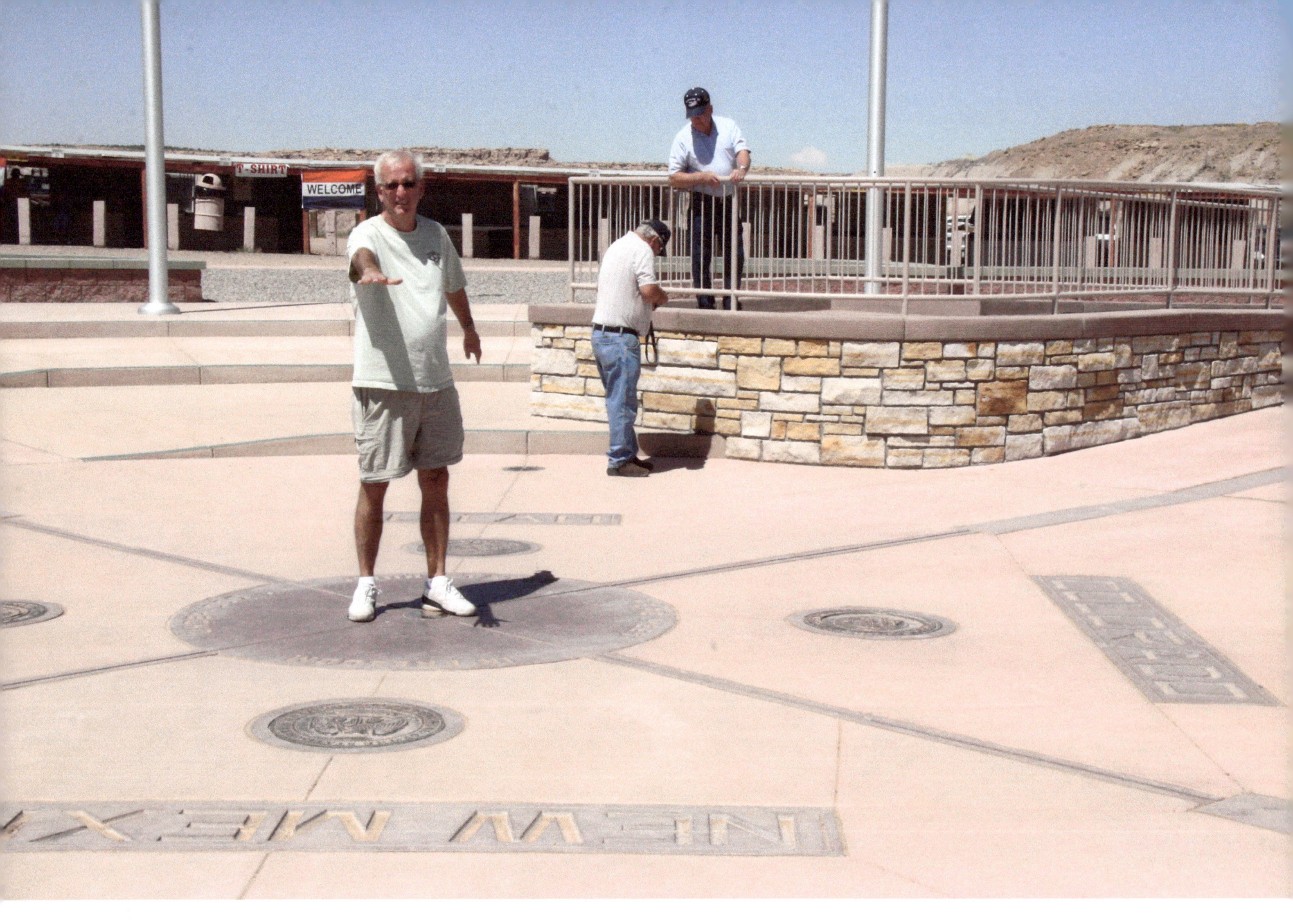

New Mexico-Reaching into the State at the Four Corners where New Mexico, Utah, Colorado and Arizona meet

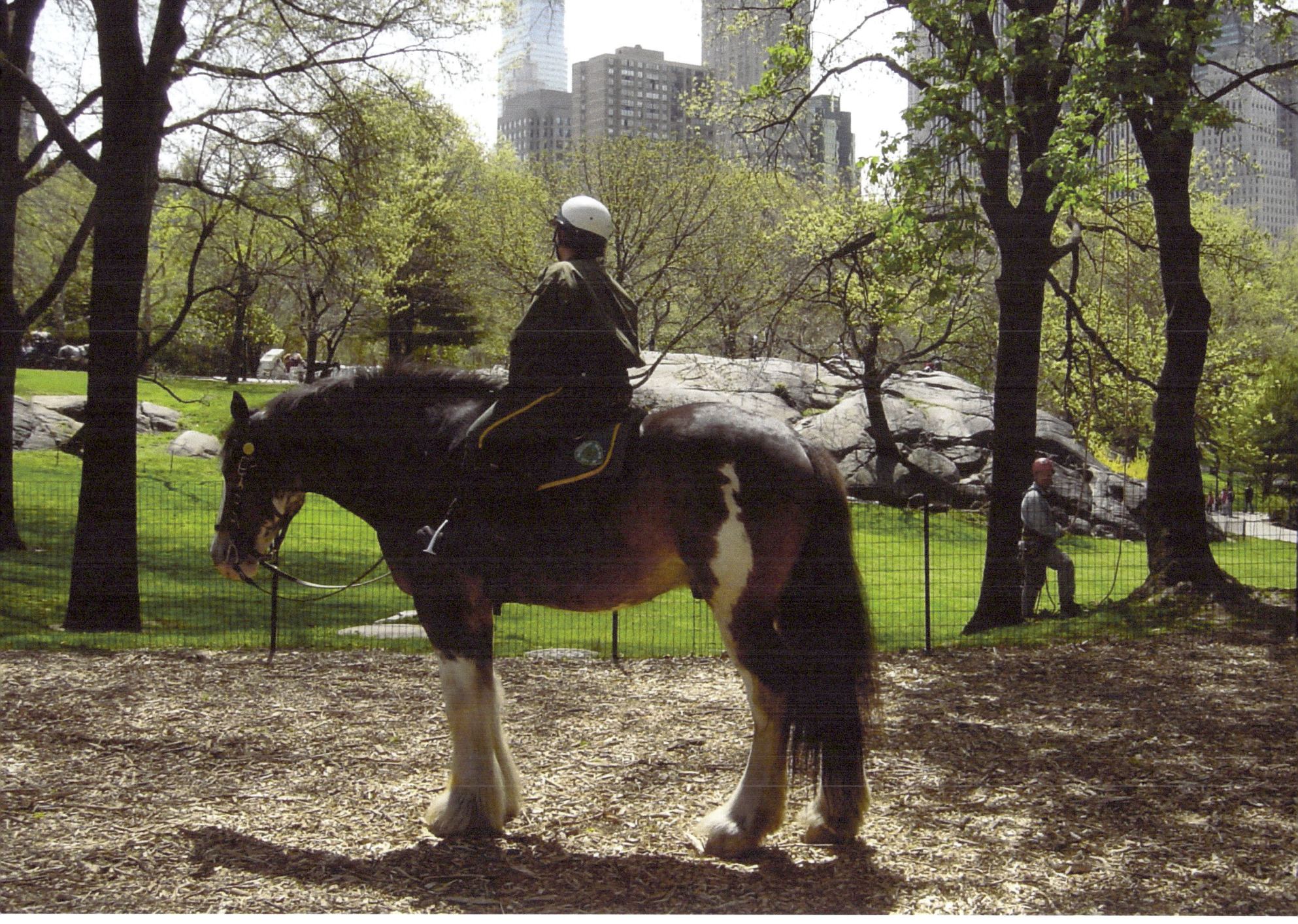

New York-Central Park

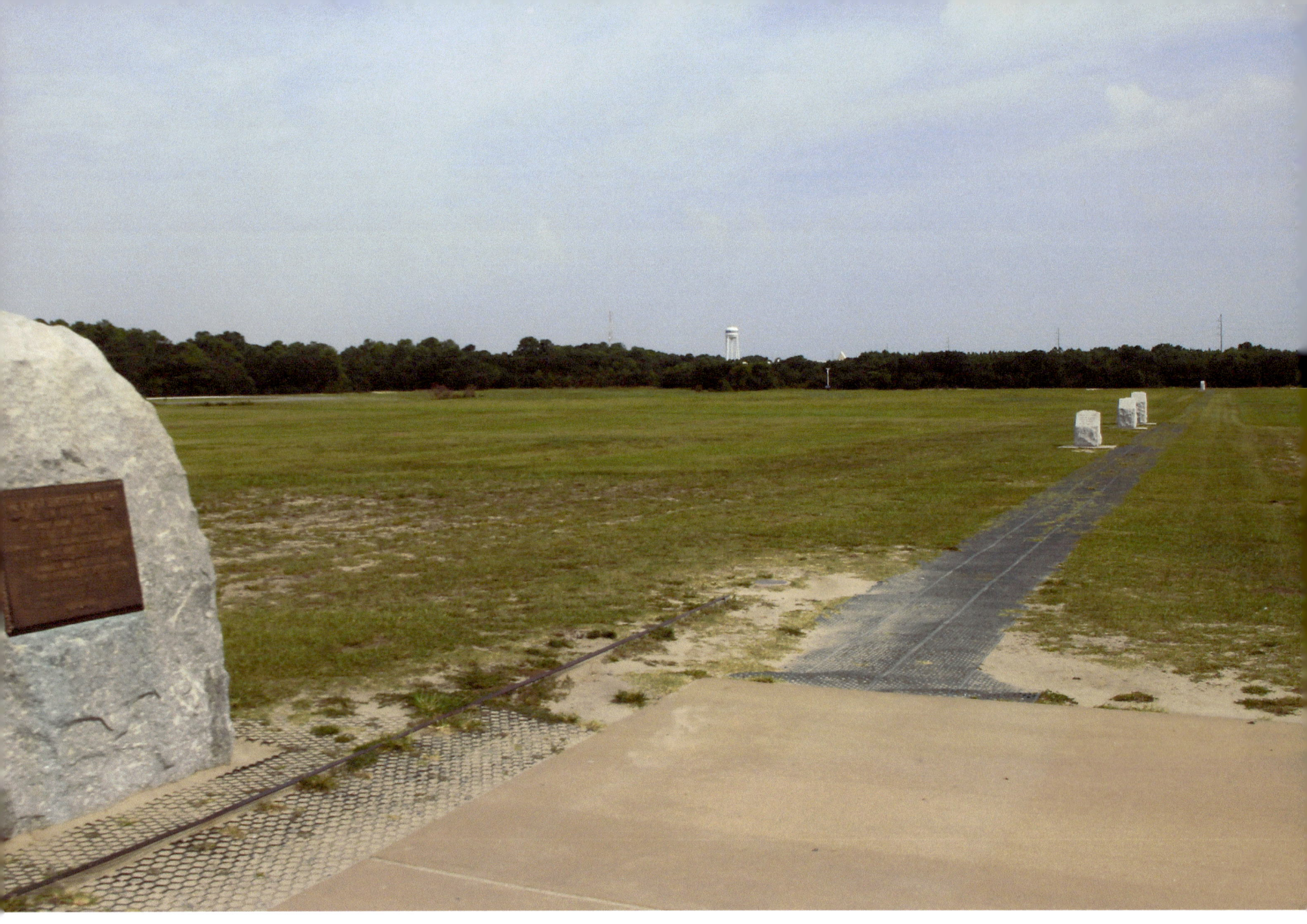

North Carolina-The markers show the first four flights of Orville and Wilbur Wright. The first flight went 120 feet, shorter than a 747-Kitty Hawk

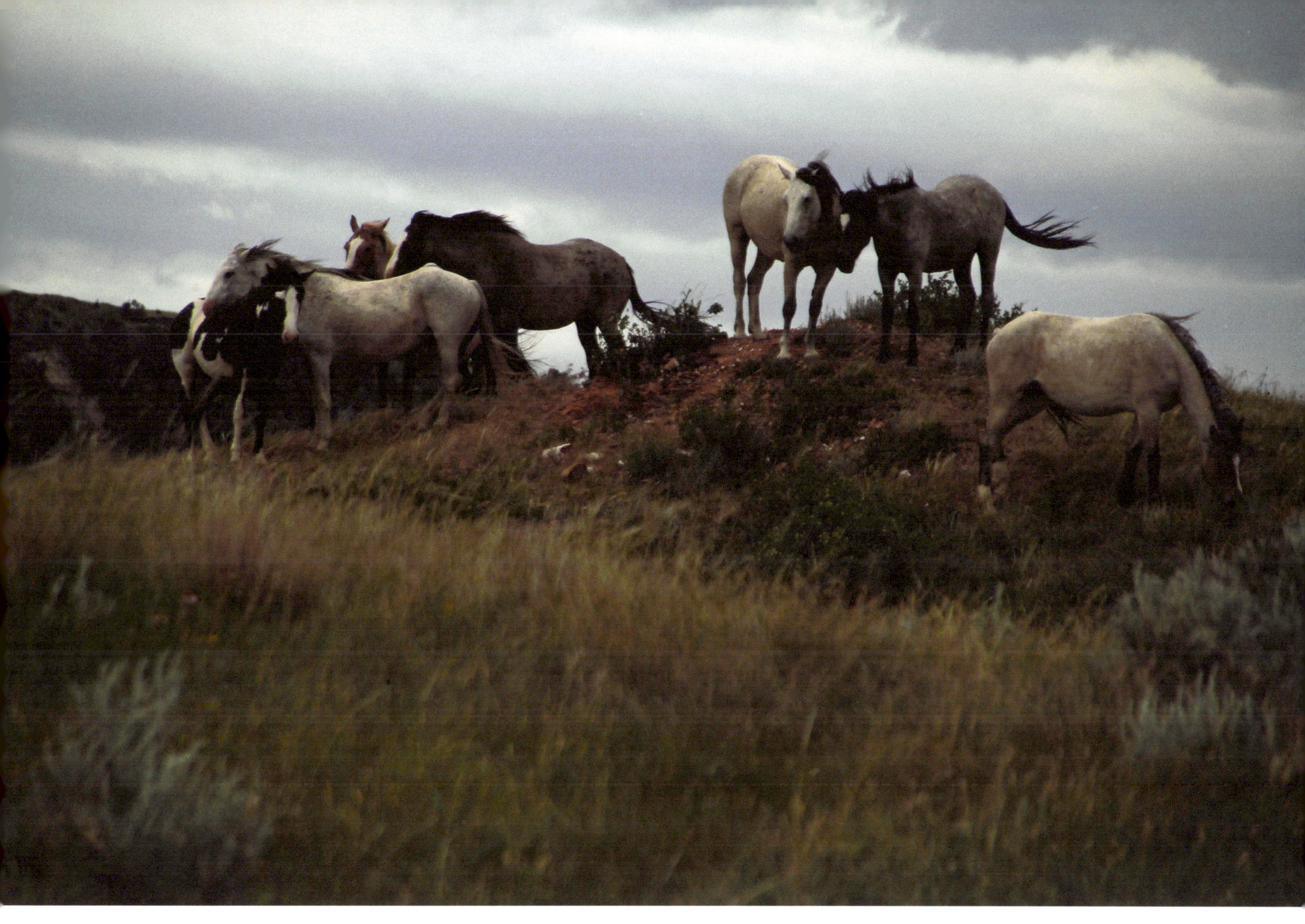

North Dakota-Feral horses in Theodore Roosevelt National Park

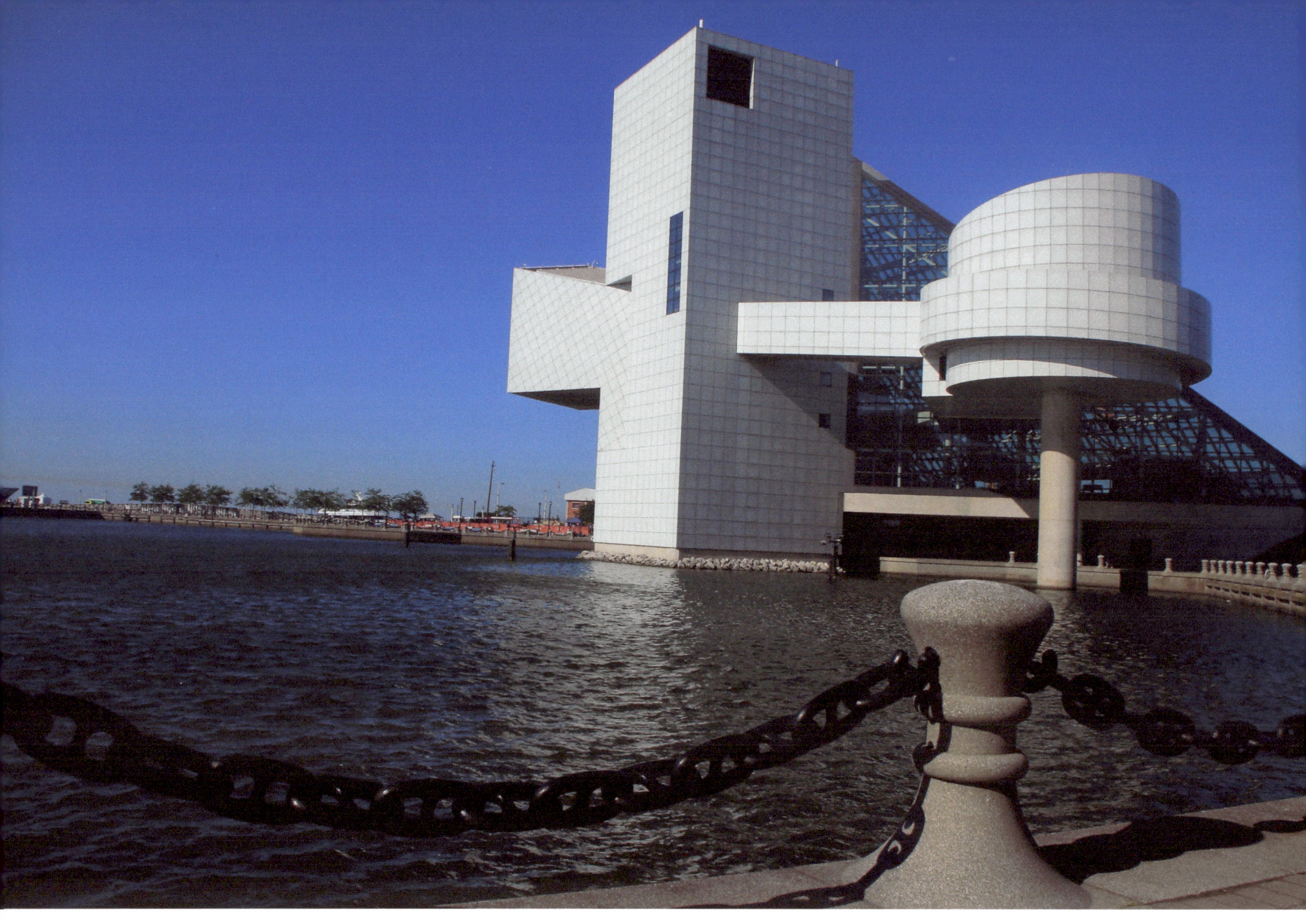

Ohio-Rock and Roll Hall of Fame on Lake Erie-Cleveland

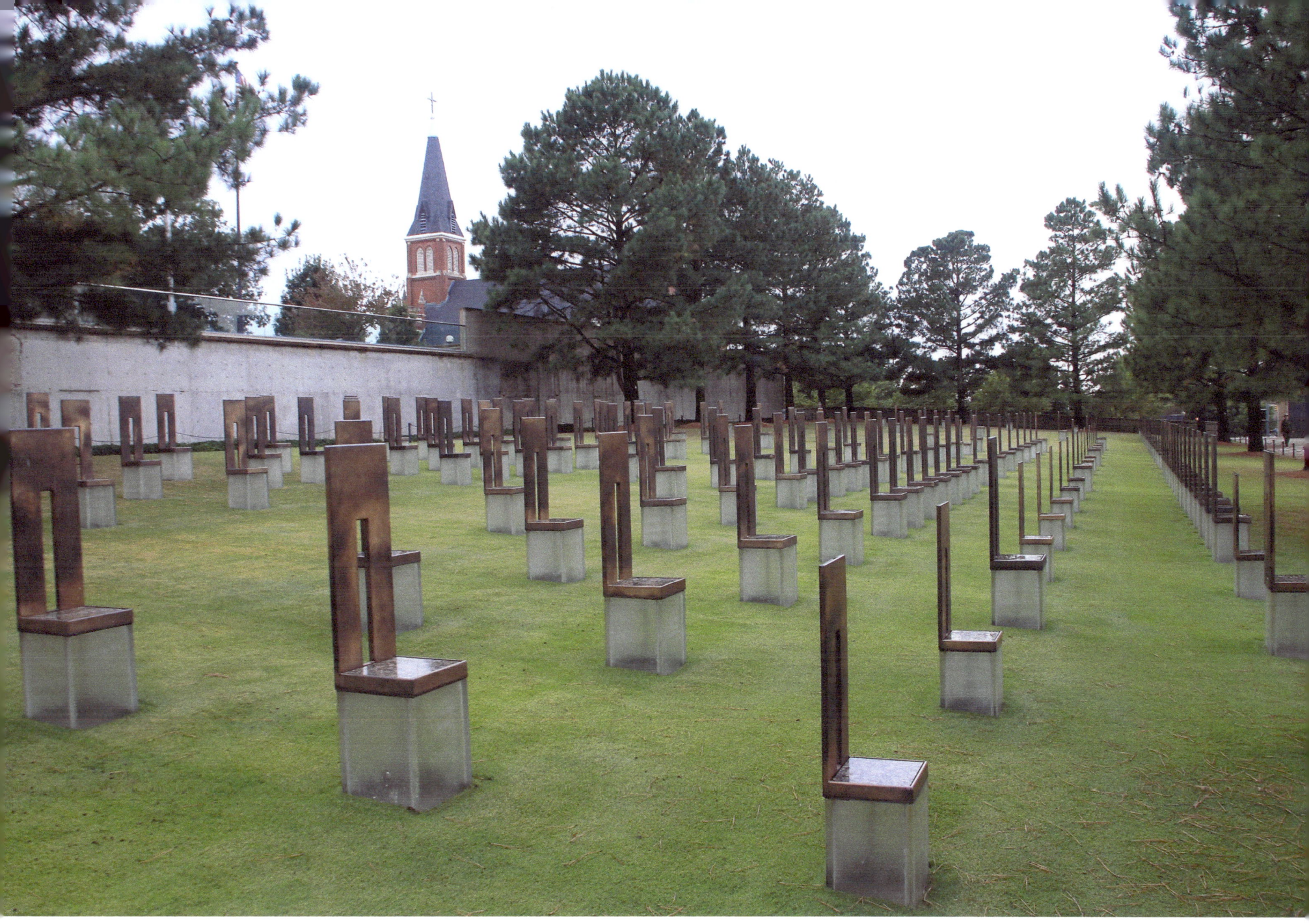

Oklahoma- This field of chairs honors the 168 people killed in the bombing of the Murrah Federal Building in 1995. Notice the shorter chairs in the second row. These honor the children killed in the day care center. Oklahoma City

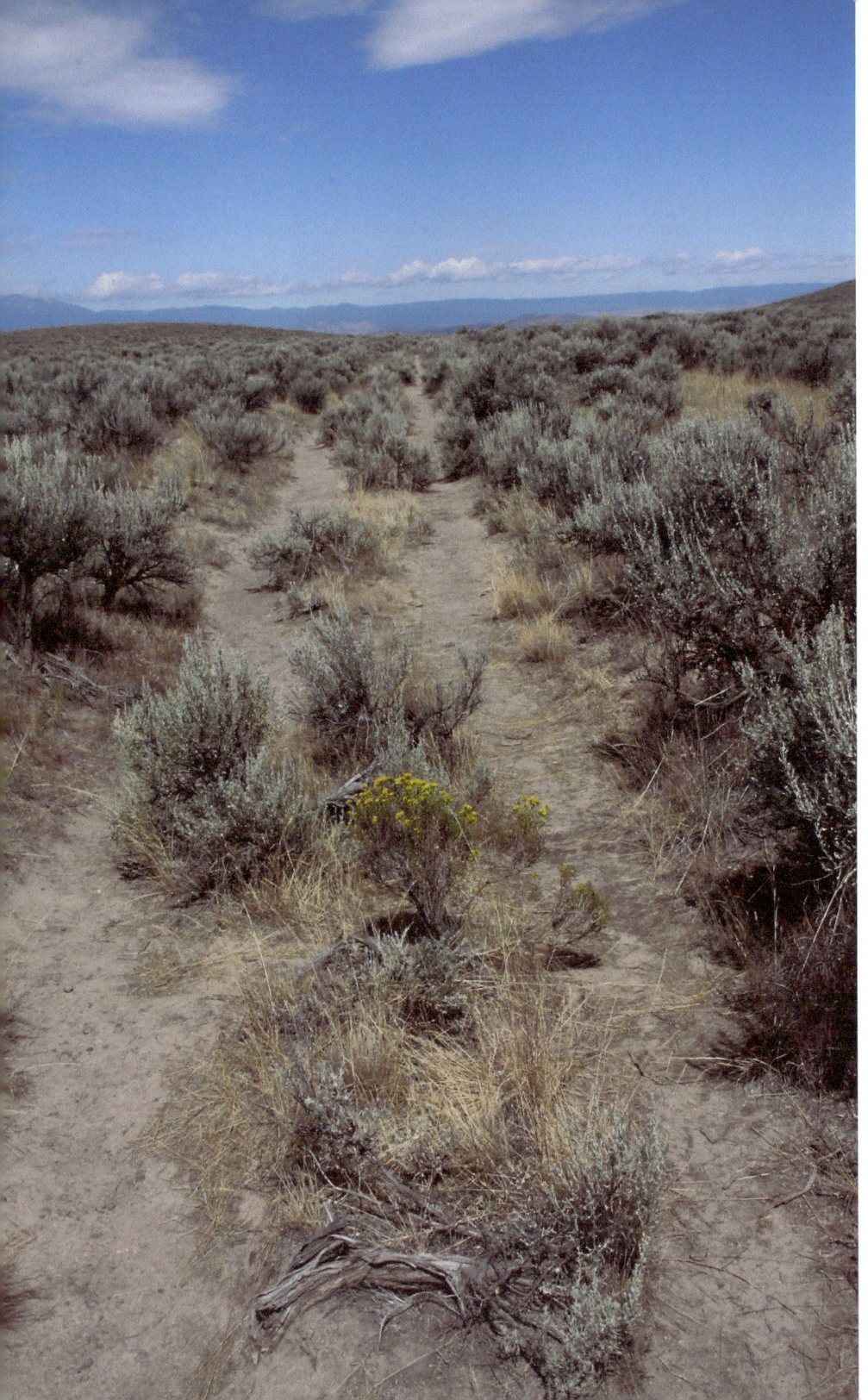

Oregon-Oregon Trail Ruts

Over 400,000 people traveled this trail over a 15 year period before the Civil War. This is considered by many scholars to be one of the largest land migrations in recorded history. Because the wagons had to be small to be pulled the 2000 miles by oxen or mules, most of the people, other than the drivers, had to walk the entire distance. Near Baker City.

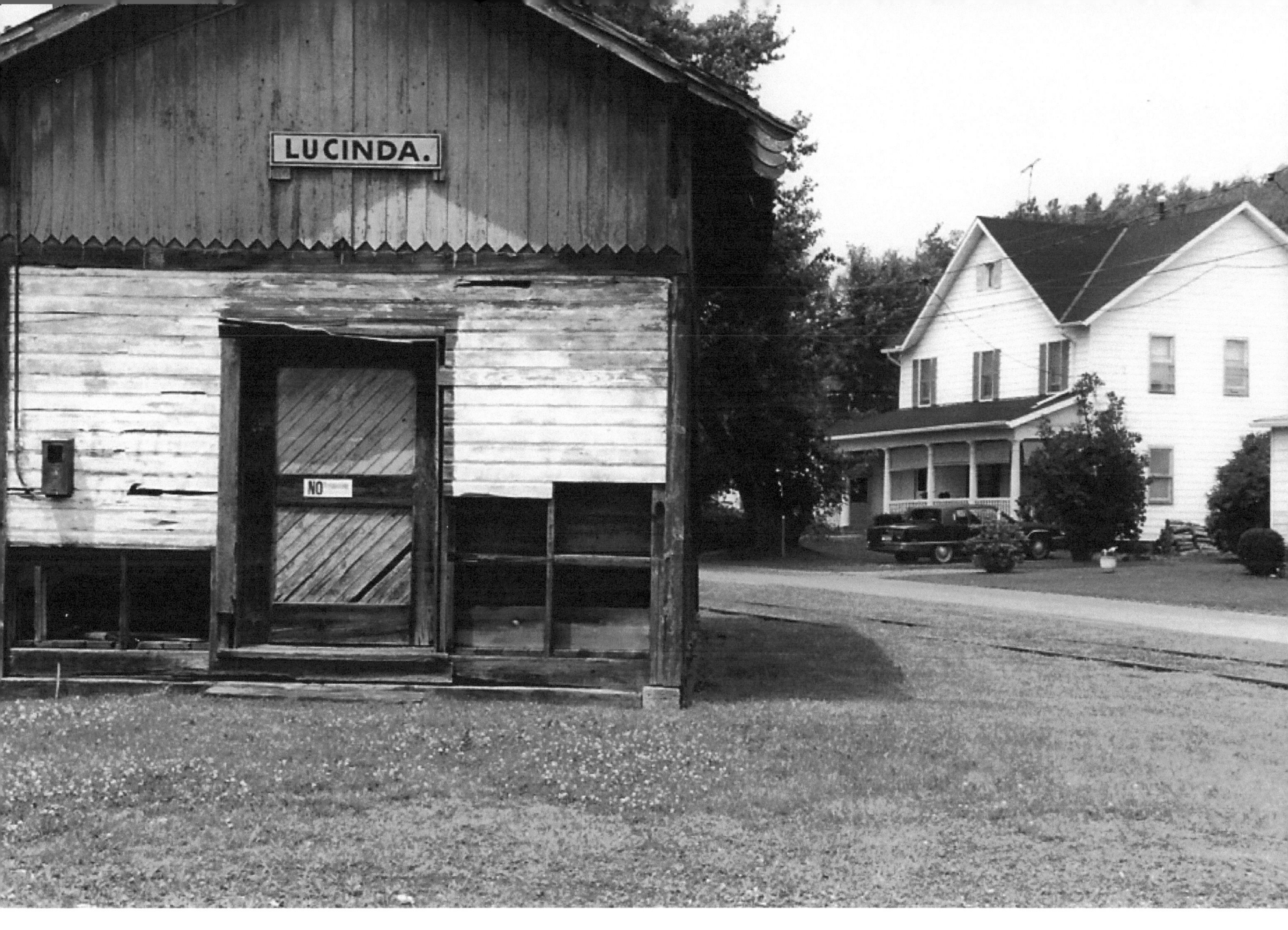

Pennsylvania-Lucinda-The original home where my mother was born is on the right

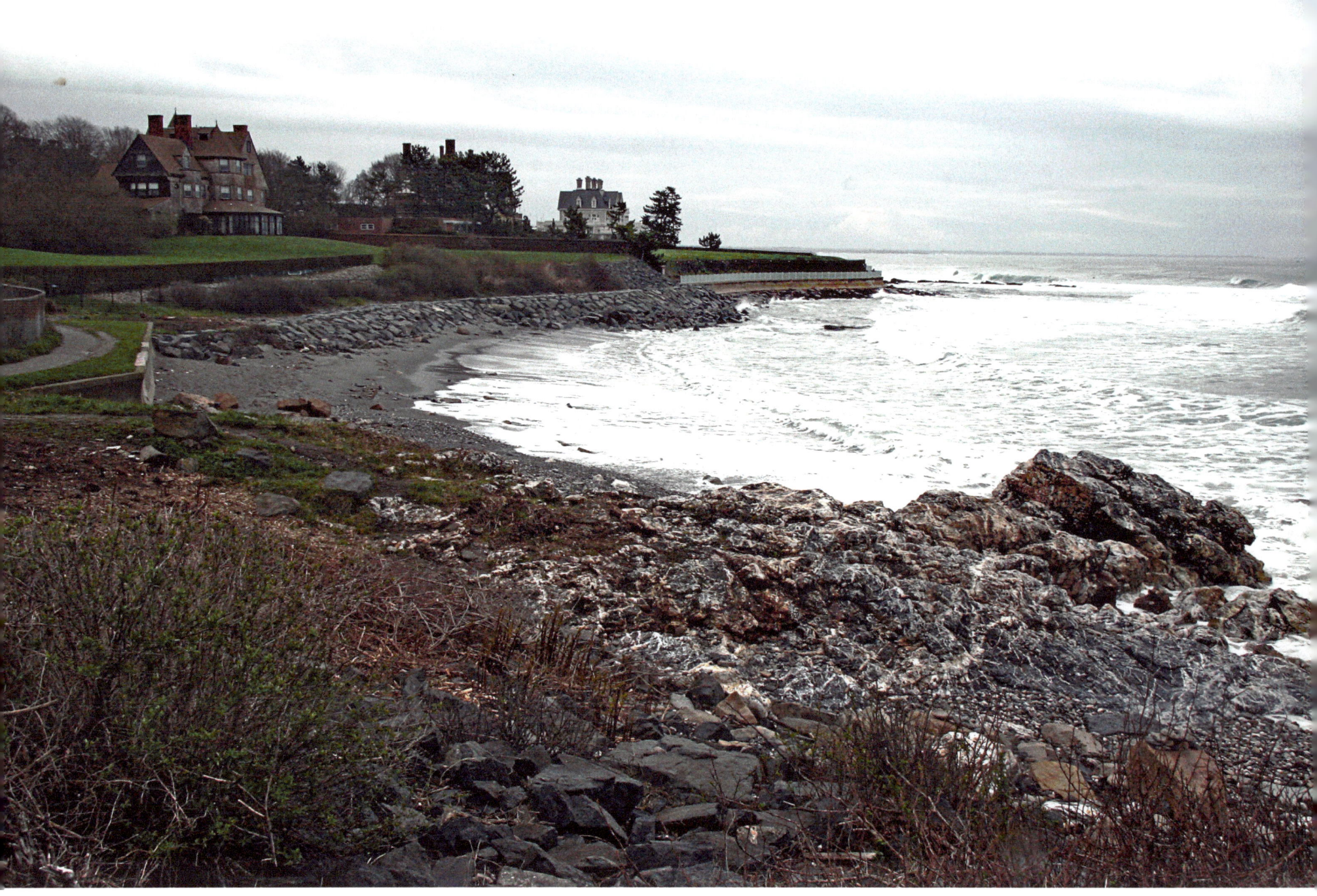

Rhode Island-Cliff Walk-Newport

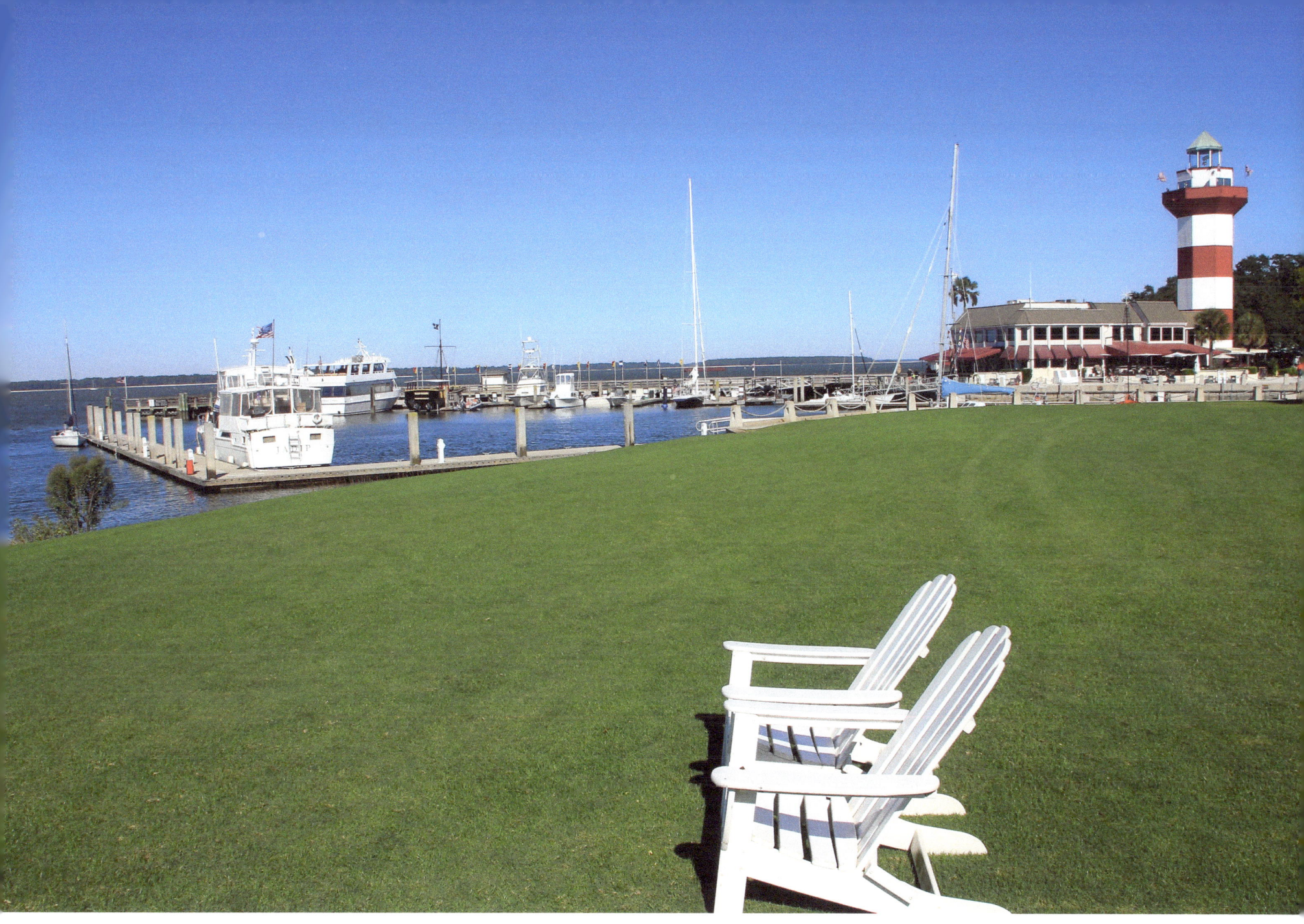

South Carolina-Hilton Head

South Dakota

The Crazy Horse Memorial is being constructed in the Black Hills. Below is the actual memorial while the upper right picture is the model for the final sculpture. The Mount Rushmore sculptures would fit on his head.

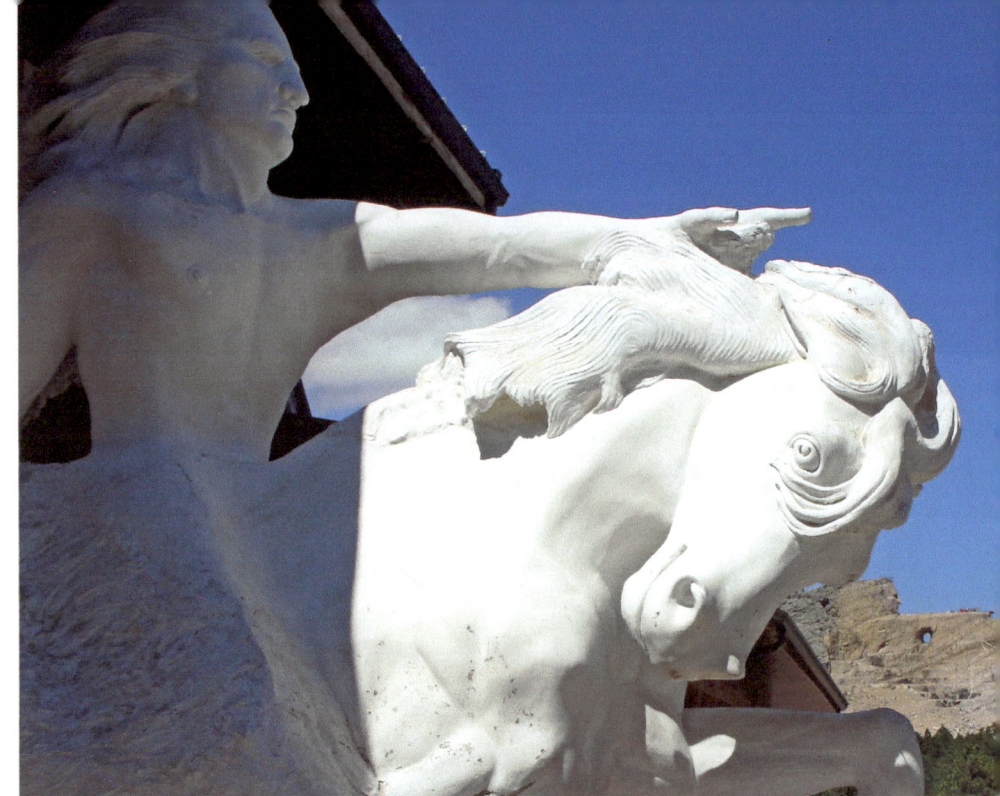

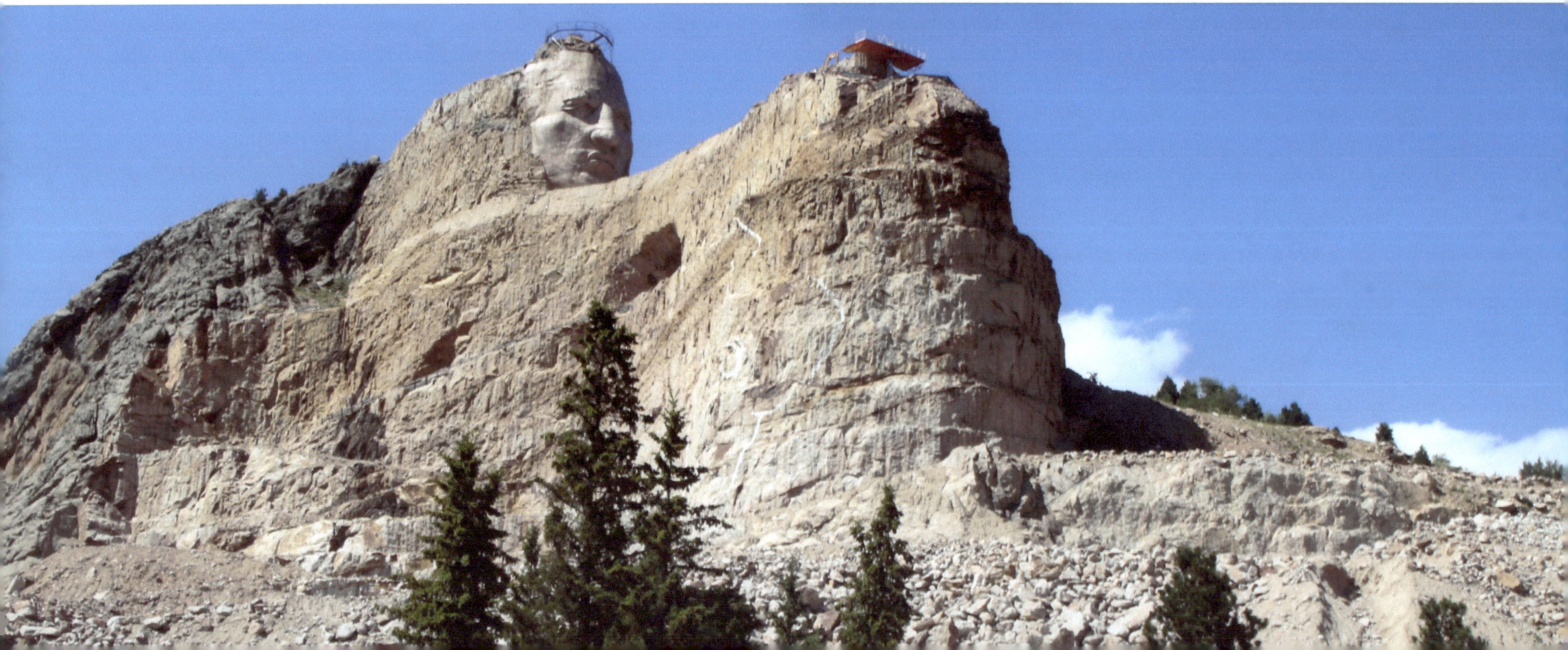

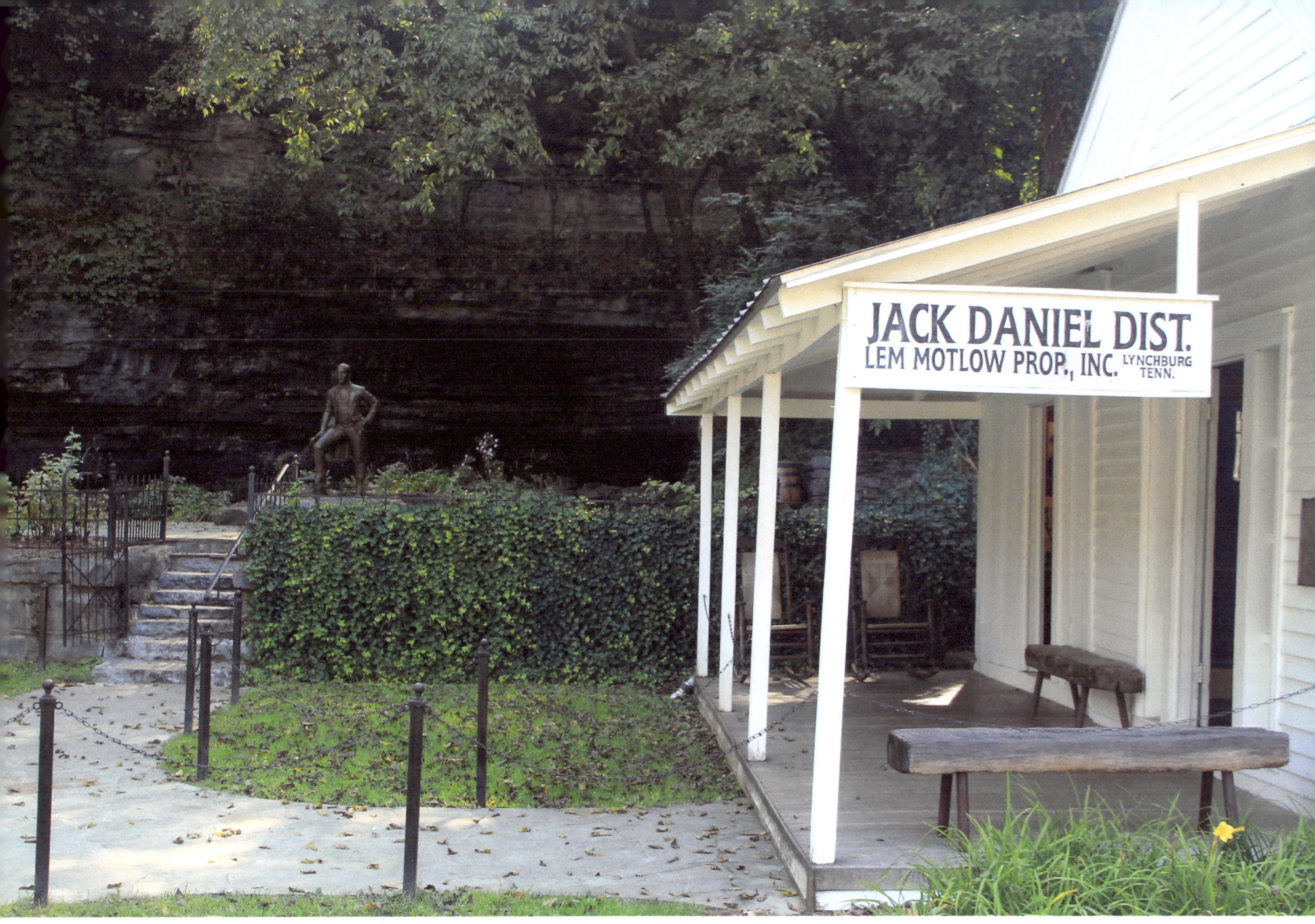

Tennessee-Jack Daniels Distillery-The original office in front of the spring and Jack on the Rocks statue-Lynchburg

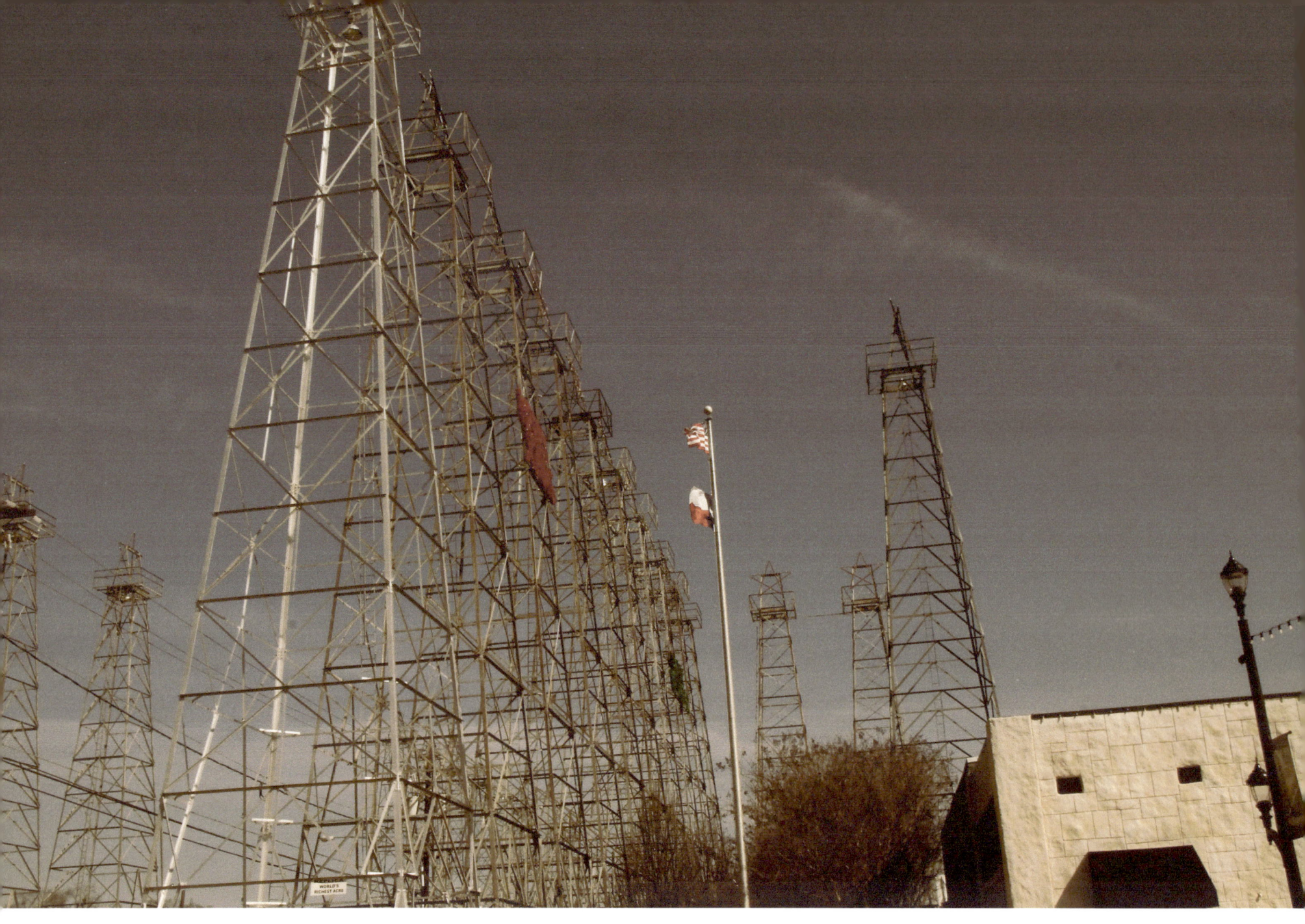

Texas-Oil Derricks in World's Richest Acre Park-Kilgore,Texas

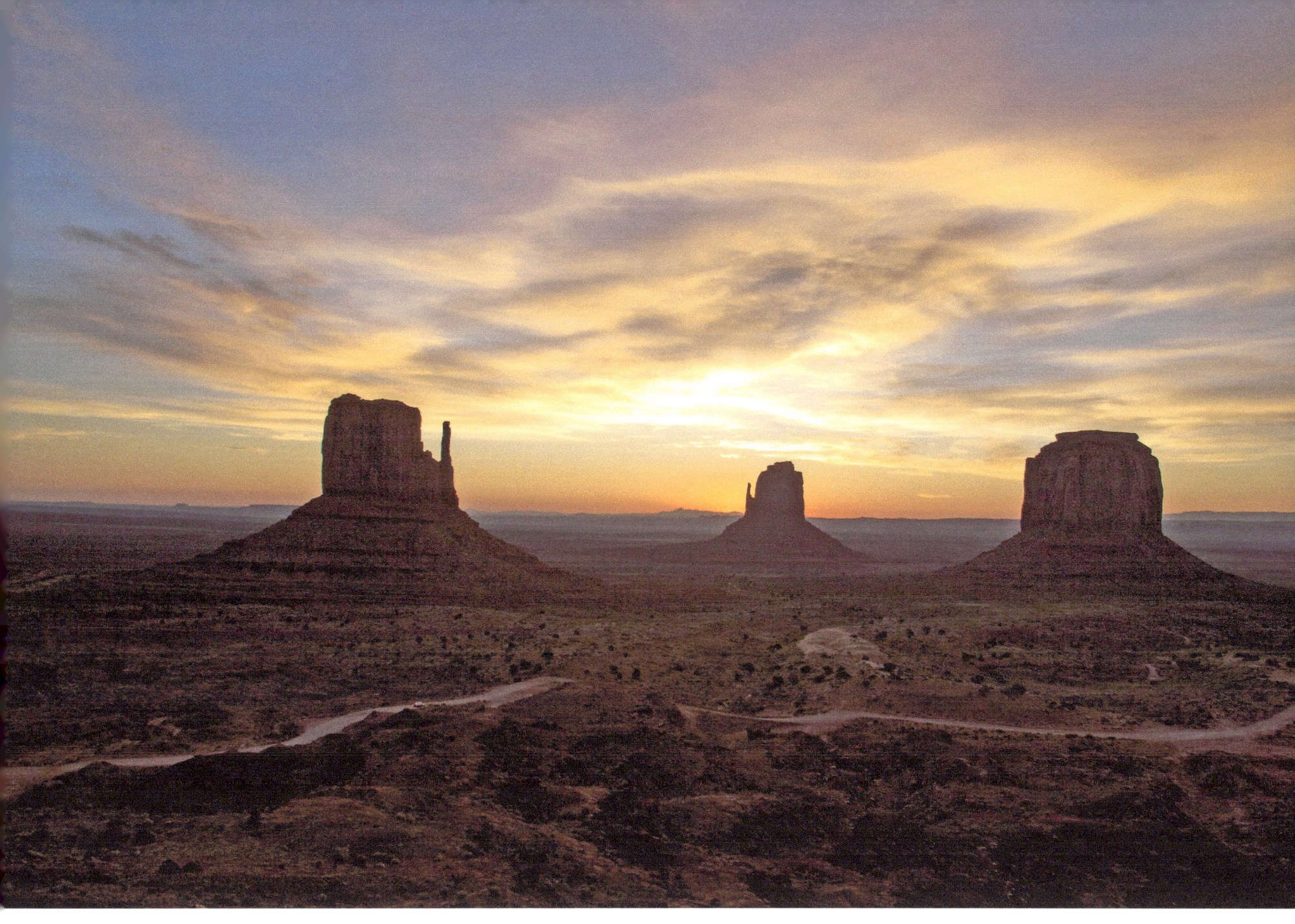

Utah-Monument Valley

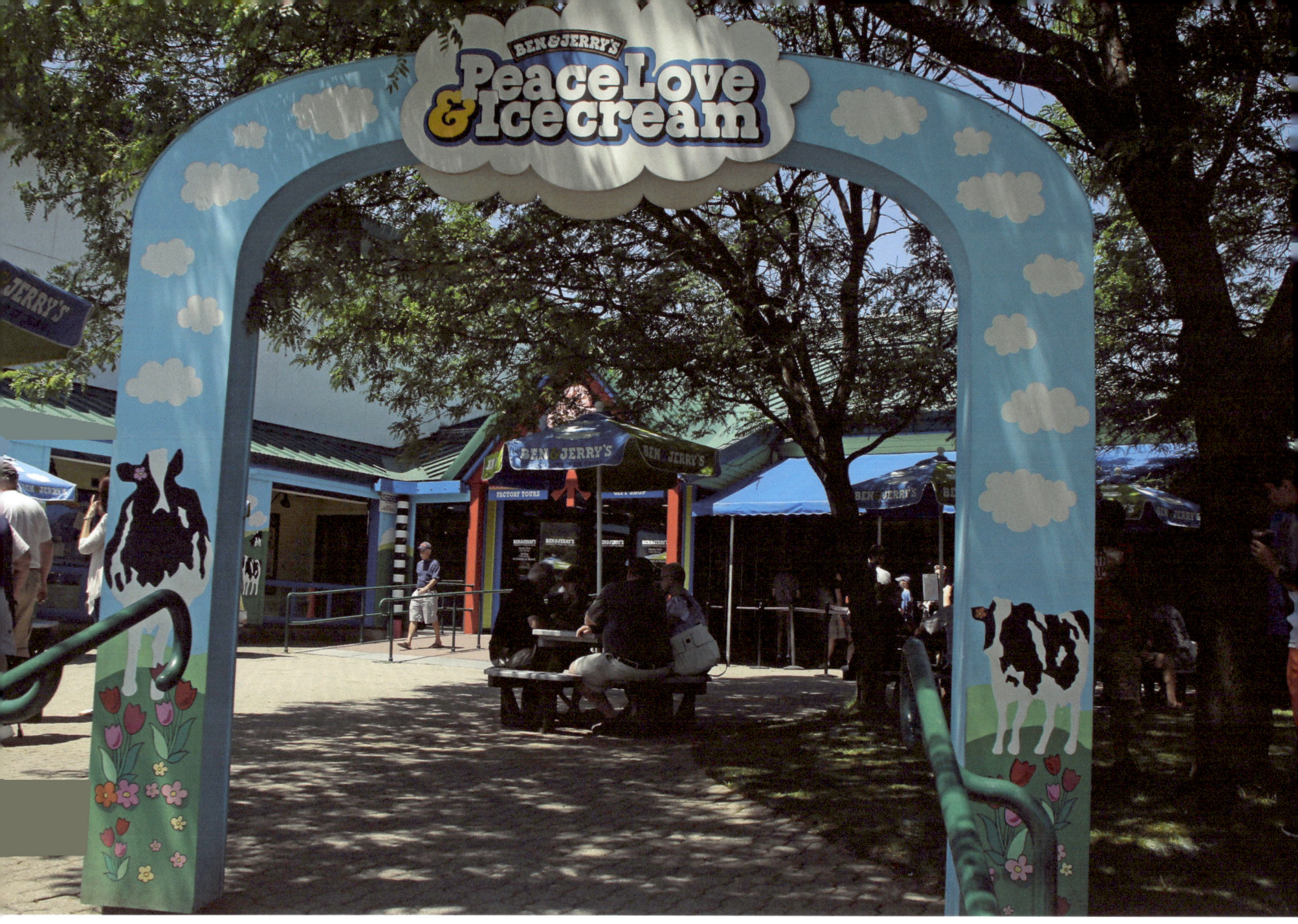

Vermont-Ben and Jerry's Factory-Stowe

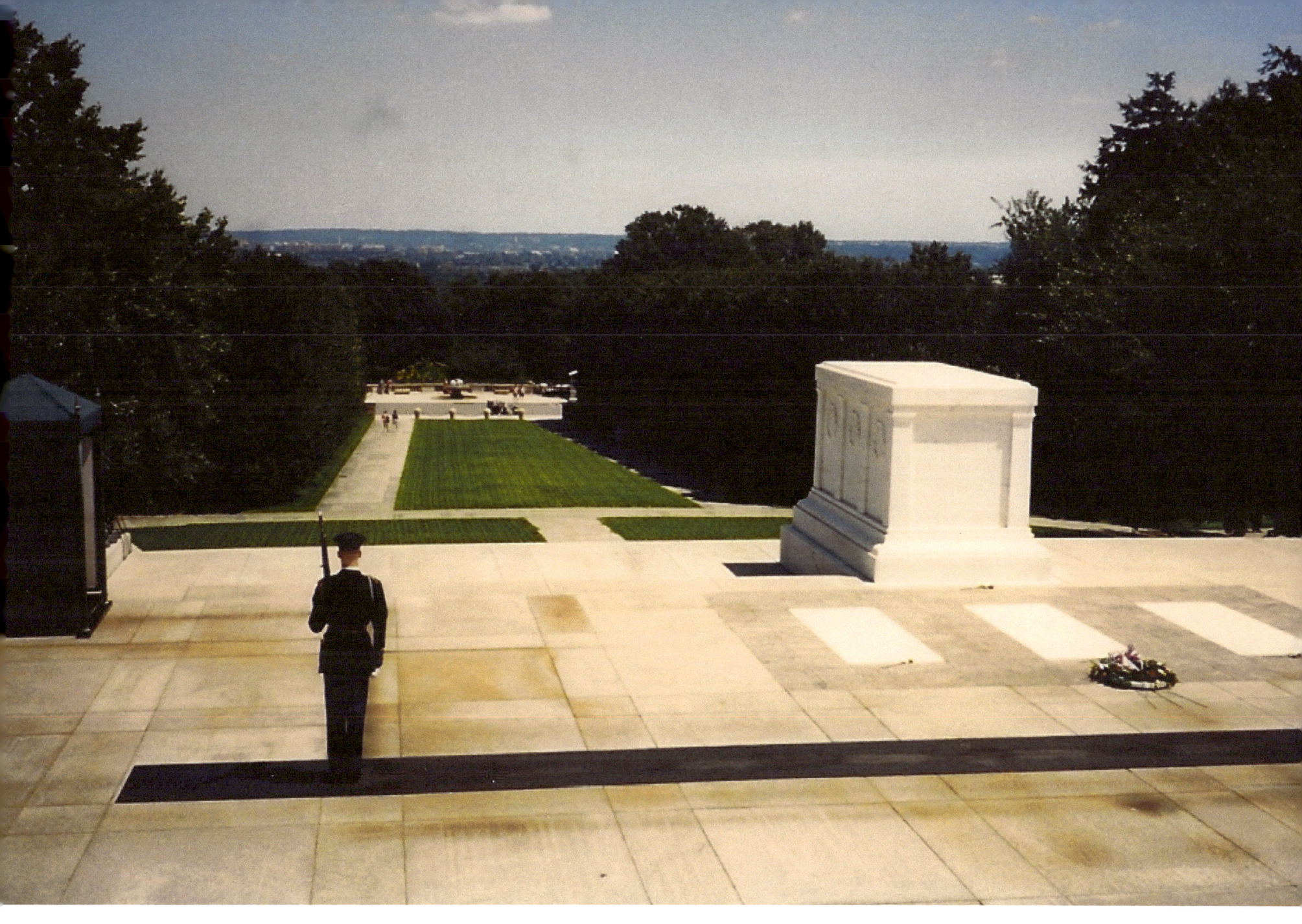

Virginia-Tomb of the Unknown-Arlington Cemetery

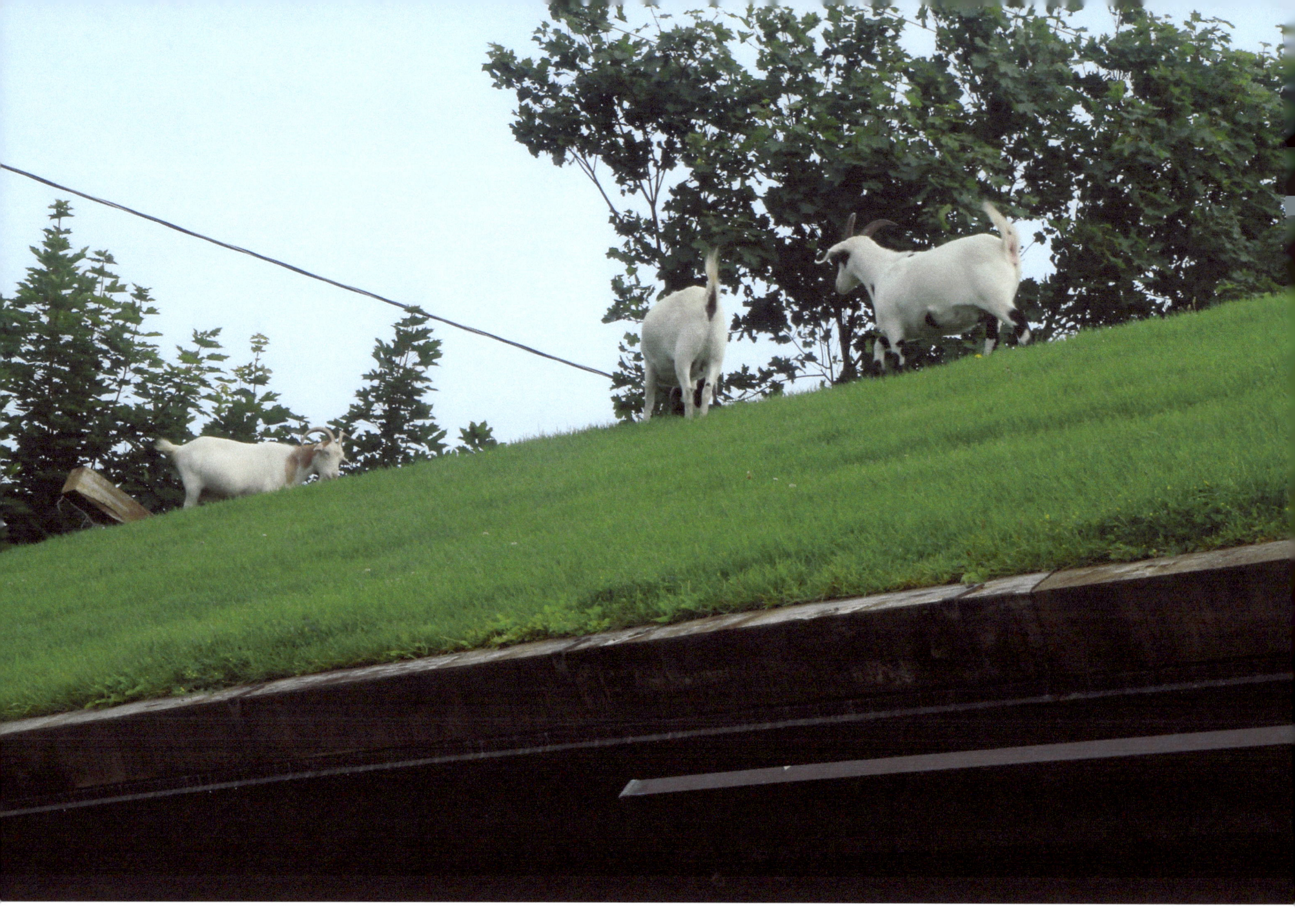

Wisconsin-Goats on the Roof-Al Johnson's Restaurant-Sister Bay

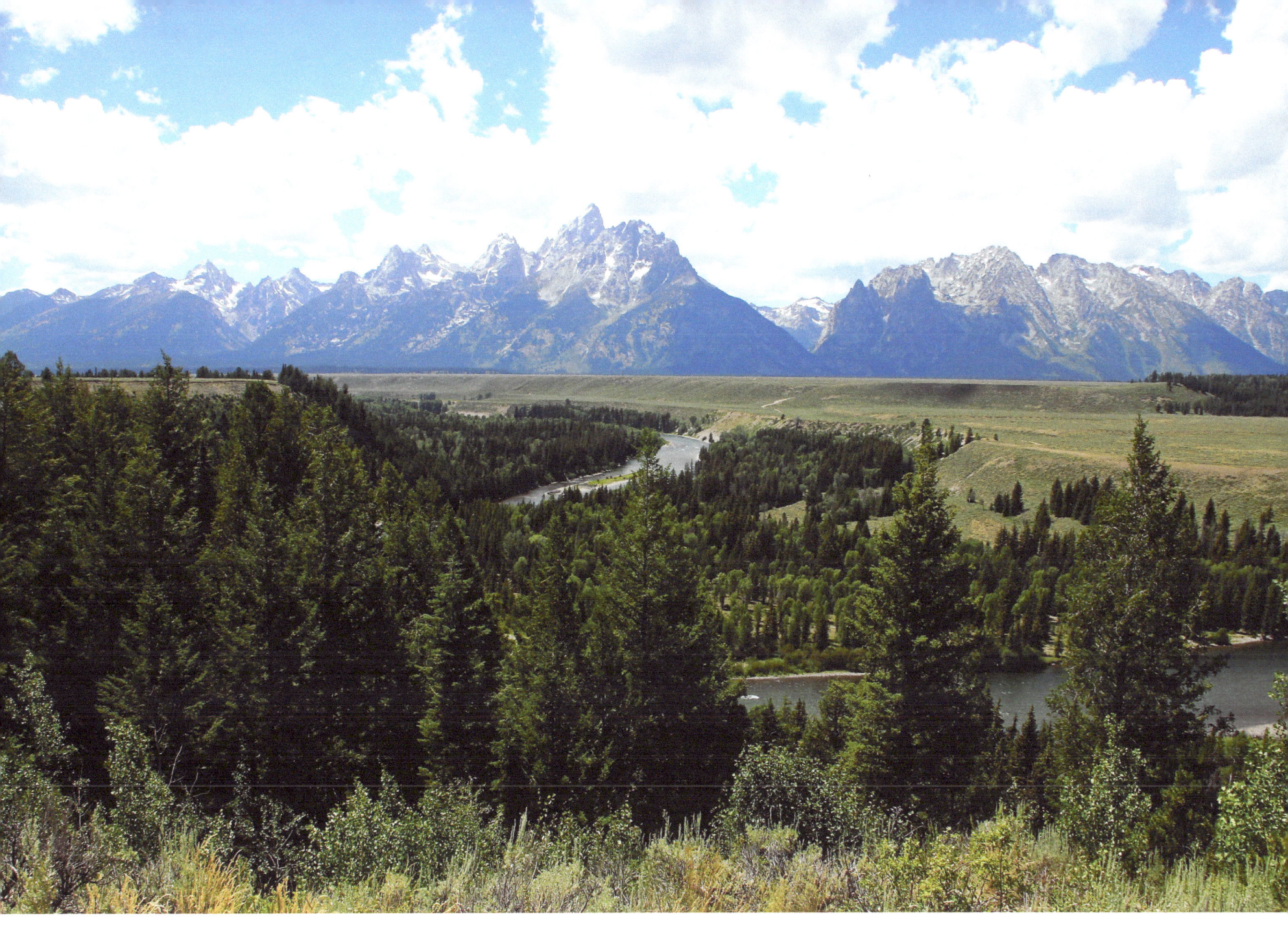

Wyoming-Grand Tetons and the Snake River

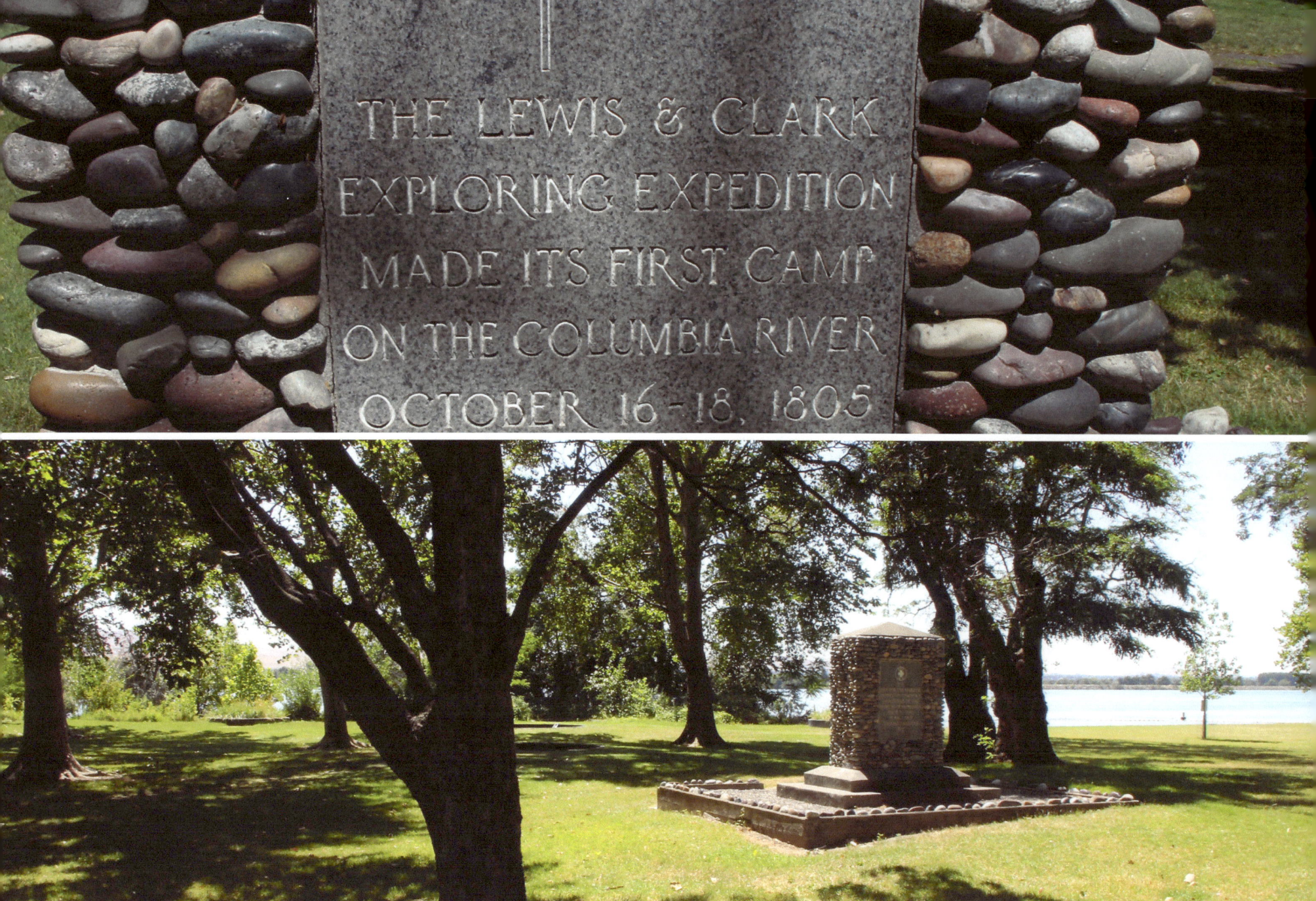

THE LEWIS & CLARK
EXPLORING EXPEDITION
MADE ITS FIRST CAMP
ON THE COLUMBIA RIVER
OCTOBER 16-18, 1805

Washington-Sacajawea State Park at the juncture of the Snake and Columbia Rivers-Lewis & Clark camped here in 1805. Because the local Indians had trinkets from The Europeans who had sailed inland on the Columbia River, they knew that they were going to make it to the Pacific-Pasco

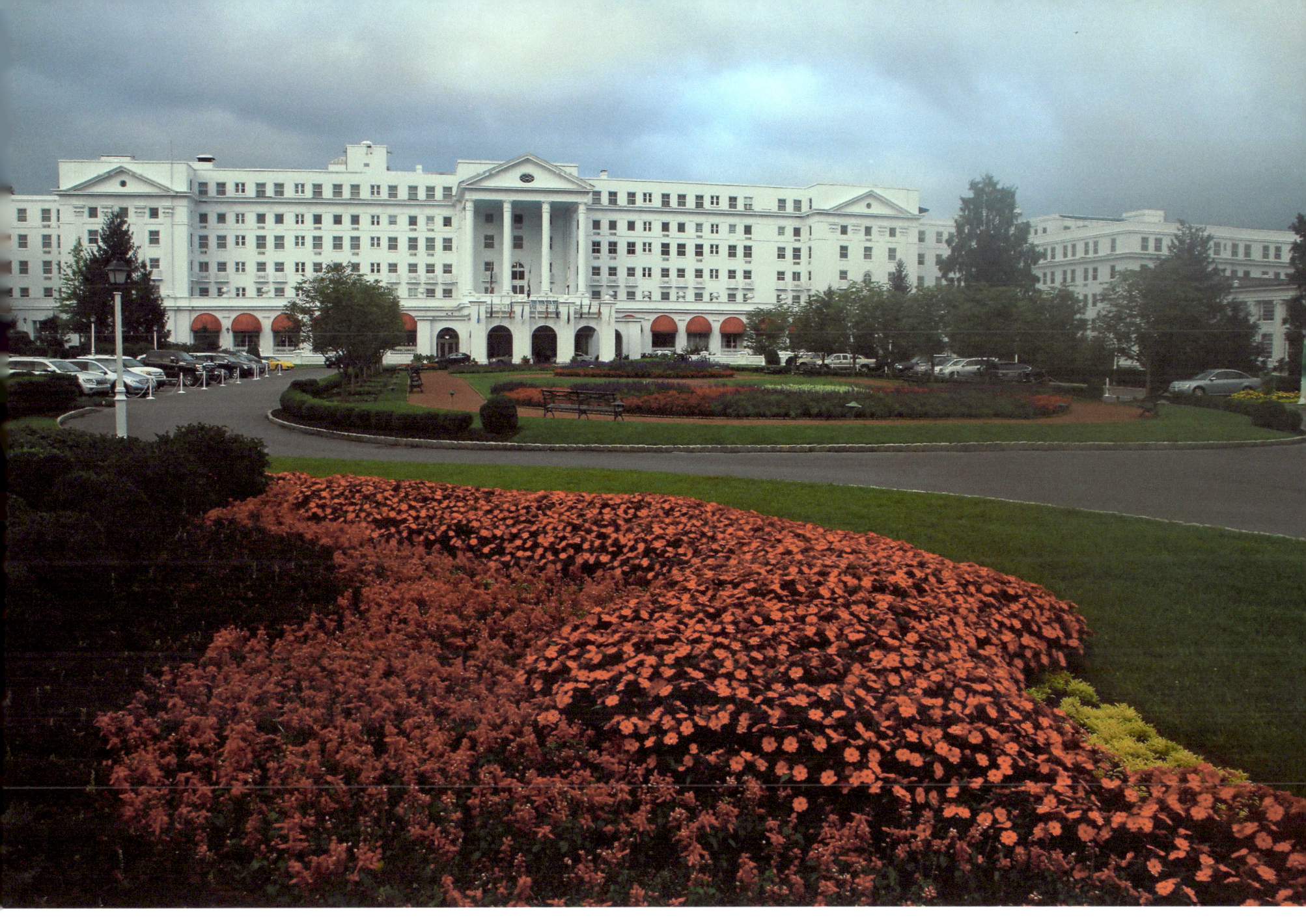

West Virginia-The Greenbrier Resort-White Sulphur Springs